FOREX TRADING

METHOD

(Strategies for Beginners to Understand the Secrets of Forex Trading)

BY

CHRIS FRANKLIN

Disclaimer

◆ ◆ ◆

All erudition contained in this book is given for informational and educational purposes only. The author is not in any way accountable for any results or outcomes that emanate from using this material. Constructive attempts have been made to provide information that is both accurate and effective, but the author is not bound for the accuracy or use/misuse of this information.

Foreword

♦ ♦ ♦

I would like to thank you for taking the first step of trusting me and deciding to purchase/read this life-transforming eBook. Thanks for spending your time and resources on this material.

I can assure you of exact results if you will diligently follow this blueprint, I lay bare in the information manual you are currently reading. It has transformed lives, and I strongly believe it will equally transform yours too.

All the information I presented in this Do It Yourself piece is easy to digest and practice.

TABLE OF CONTENTS

INTRODUCTION

◆ ◆ ◆

Forex trading for beginners can be especially extraordinary. This is generally a result of absurd wants that are typical among newcomers. What you can make certain of is that cash trading is by no means a fraudulent business model. In this section, you will get an introduction to the Forex Market; how it works, and the benefits of trading different currencies.

We can cover how you can start trading (checking picking the best dealer and trading programming), the nuts and bolts of risk the administrators, the different ways you can separate the Forex Market, and an audit of the most conspicuous trading frameworks. Before the completion of this guide, you will have the data you need to start testing your trading capacities with a free Demo account, before you move on to trading real cash.

What is Forex?

Forex or the Foreign Exchange Market (moreover called FX for short), is the business focus where currencies are traded. A remote exchange trade might be, for example, when you move your local money to another for an imminent event. Over the market with everything taken into account, a normal 5.3 billion USD is traded every day between governments, banks, and analysts.

Knowing how the business works is huge, in light of the way that the total mix of all currencies make up the market..

Which Forex Pairs Can You Trade?

Forex pairs are known as majors, minors, and exotics.

There are a great number of pairs that can be traded on the market. Below are the major currencies traded on Forex:

- USD - The US Dollar
- EUR - The Euro
- JPY - The Japanese Yen
- GBP - The British Pound
- CHF - The Swiss Franc
- CAD - The Canadian Dollar
- AUD - The Australian Dollar
- NZD - The New Zealand Dollar

A major pair is one that contains any of these fiscal structures coordinated against the US dollar, for instance, the EUR/USD, USD/JPY or the GBP/USD. Forex minors sets made up of these noteworthy money related structures that do bar the US dollar. These sets include EUR/GBP, EUR/CHF, AUD/NZD, and so on.

Finally, unprecedented financial principles are any money related norms that we haven't quite recently referenced, for instance, the Hong Kong Dollar (HKD), the Norwegian Krone (NOK), the South African Rand (ZAR) and the Thai Baht (THB). When starting out in Forex trading, various amateurs will focus on major cash sets because of their step by step capriciousness and tight spreads. However, there are different possibilities – from uncommon FX sets, to CFD trading openings on stocks, imperativeness destinies, and accounts. There are even accounts that track social occasions of accounts, and you can trade them too.

The number of instruments you look at for investment is up to you. However, don't limit yourself to just one instrument or one market. Market limitation can provoke overtrading, so attempt to expand your endeavor.

How Do Forex Quotes Work?

When trading Forex, you'll see that both 'Offer' and 'Ask' costs are referred to. The offer expense is the expense at which you can buy the cash, while the ask cost is the expense at which you can sell it. If you are getting a cash in a trade, this is known as a long trade, and the desire is that the money pair will increase in worth, with the objective that you can sell it at a progressively noteworthy cost and have an advantage on the impact.

If you are selling a money in a trade, the reverse is legitimate - the desire is that the cash pair will fall in worth, with the objective that you can repurchase it at a lower cost, which means you will profit on the differentiation.

The number referred to at these expenses relies upon the present swapping size of the financial principles in the pair, or the measure of the second cash you would receive as an end-result of one unit of the chief money (for instance, if 1 EUR could be exchanged for 1.68 USD, the offer and ask cost would be on either side of this number). Study the section Understanding and Reading Forex Quotes to better understand this.

SETTING UP A TRADER ACCOUNT

Forex Basics: Setting Up an Account

Remote exchange (forex) trading involves obtaining and selling world money related norms, and the business focus is among the most liquid on earth. Forex trading is remarkable in light of the way that individual monetary masters can fight with gigantic multifaceted speculations and banks—they just need to set up the right account.

There are three types of trading accounts—standard, little scale, and directed—and each has its own special pros and cons. Which type is best for you depends on your opposition for risk, the size of your hidden hypothesis, and the amount of time you have to trade each day.

Standard Trading Accounts

The standard trading account is the most broadly perceived. This account gives the customer access to money worth $100,000.

That doesn't infer that you have to put down $100,000 of income to trade. The rules of edge and impact (customarily 100:1 in forex) suggest that just $1,000 ought to be in the edge speak to one standard package to be traded.

The Pros

Organization: Because the standard account requires adequate ahead of time cash to trade full packages, most authorities give more organizations and better focal points for individual money related experts who have this sort of account.

Increment Potential: With each pip worth $10, if a position moves by 100 pips in a solitary day, the expansion will be $1,000.

The Cons

Capital Requirement: Most go-betweens require standard accounts to have a starting capital of $2,000 and some $5,000 to $10,000.

Adversity Potential

Thus as you get the opportunity to get $1,000 if a position moves with you, you could lose $1,000 in a 100-pip move against you. This setback could be squashing to a fresh intermediary with just the base in an account.

This kind of account is recommended for experienced, well-financed sellers.

Littler than typical Trading Accounts

A littler than typical trading account is essentially a trading account that empowers representatives to make trades using little bundles. In most currency market reserves, a littler than normal package is comparable to $10,000, or one-tenth of a standard account. Most traders offering standard accounts will similarly offer littler than ordinary accounts as a way to deal with get new clients who are hesitant to trade full bundles because of the capital required.

The Pros

By and large sheltered: By trading $10,000 increments, fresh agents can trade without blowing through their accounts, and experienced sellers can test new methods without betting a great deal of capital.

Low Capital Requirement: Most littler than anticipated accounts can be opened with $250 to $500, and they go with impact of up to 400:1.

Versatility: The best approach to productive trading is having a risk plan and holding fast to it. With littler than regular shares, this is a lot more straightforward as compared to the standard package which is higher risked; you can buy five or six downsized shares and farthest point your risk.

The Cons

Low Reward

With alright comes low reward. Littler than ordinary accounts that trade $10,000 shares can simply convey $1 per pip of advancement instead of $10 in a standard accounts. This kind of account is endorsed for amateur forex traders or those wanting to dillydally with new techniques.

Littler scale accounts, the sister account to the little, are also open through some online delegates. These accounts trade $1,000 shares and have pip improvements worth 10 pennies for each point. These trading accounts are consistently used for money related authorities with compelled outside exchange data and can be opened for as small as $25.

Managed Trading Account

Managed trading accounts are forex accounts in which the capital is yours, however, the decisions to buy and sell are certainly not. Account executives handle the account also as stockbrokers handle a managed stock account, where you set the goals (advantage destinations, risk the board) and the boss work to meet them.

There are two sorts of coordinated trading accounts:

1. Pooled Funds: Your cash is placed into a normal store with that of different analysts, and the preferences are shared. These accounts are described by risk adaptability. An authority searching for continuously significant yields would place their cash into a pooled account that has a higher risk/repay degree while a dealer checking for a determined pay would do the opposite. Investigate the spare's course of action before contributing.

2. Individual Accounts: A trader will manage each account freely, choosing decisions for each monetary authority as opposed to the joined pool.

The Pros

Capable Guidance: Having a specialist forex trader handle an account is a touch of breathing space that can't be misrepresented. Moreover, in case you have to grow your portfolio without experiencing for the duration of the day watching the market, this is an exceptional choice.

The Cons

Cost: Note that most supervised accounts will require a base $2,000 adventure for pooled accounts and $10,000 for individual accounts. Over this, account manager will keep a commission, called an account bolster cost, which is paid each month or consistently.

Freedom: If you see the market moving, you won't have the versatility to put a position. Or maybe, you'll have to rely upon the account director to choose the right share. This kind of account is proposed for money related experts with high capital and no time or excitement to seek after the market.

The Bottom Line

Notwithstanding, what account type you choose, must be based on an assessment first. Most go-betweens offer demo accounts, which offer money related experts an opportunity to use an account risk free and assess different stages and organizations.

As a fundamental rule, never put money into a account aside from the off chance that you are absolutely content with the predictions being made. With the different options open for forex trading accounts, the difference between being advantageous and ending up in the red may be as direct as picking the right account.

STEPS TO COMPLETE A SUCCESSFULL TRADE

Trading JOURNAL

Keeping a trading journal is a splendid system to improve execution and increment trust in executions. Achievement in forex trading requires a noteworthy degree of orchestrating and practice. To be dependably successful in trading, forex dealers need to encounter a careful learning process. The best instrument to oversee and propel a forex seller's structure is utilizing a trading journal. In case you plan on transforming into a powerful agent through execution, trading journals can guide you much speedier towards a helpful calling.

What is a trading journal?

A trading journal is perhaps the best gadget for young traders. It is where you record and review step by step trades for better yield and for future reference. A journal can empower you to track progress similarly as study blunders made when entering or leaving a trade. As time goes on, these reports can go about as the foundation for better executions.

Points of interest of having a trading journal:

With a trading journal, forex vendors can develop a useful system reliant on trading foundation. After some time, the inclinations are significant for trading adequacy. Expecting dependably and constantly revived, your trading journal will be the best approach to positive trades.

Manufactures mindful structure for systems

Compelling trading relies upon an advantageous framework where you can develop your methods. Through demanding record of material nuances, all tallies and moves made during the trade session can be fittingly assessed. This framework can choose the achievement of your trades and can avoid future difficulties for a dynamically impeccable trading method.

Directs excited triggers

A compelling calling in forex trading has a lot to do with mind science and mental state. Most forex agents experience certain inclination that could provoke off the cuff exercises. Having a trading journal empowers you to watch all that you felt and picked up from a trade. This preparation enables you to perceive your considerations and eager triggers behind each trade.

Portrays your characteristics and deficiencies

Filing each trade can help portray your characteristics and weaknesses as a forex vendor. Through these observations, you can be your very own advisor and brace better trading capacities. Journaling, in like manner, permits you be progressively liable for any errors. By perceiving what you have some expertise in or what requires more noteworthy improvement, you can upgrade your trading aptitudes and build them into your trading system.

Keeps you out of a scrappy trade

Having a trading journal is a phenomenal strategy to stick to a trading plan. Most traders will, as a rule, lose money in the forex exhibit because of offhand moves or hasty trades. Watching these sorts of trades can hold your sentiments and decisions under tight limitations and can empower you to end up being dynamically aware of the potential results. In the wake of creating a sound trading plan, use a trading journal to keep you out of sketchy trades.

Stimulates execution driven advancement

The more assessment you make from your trading journal, the better you can adjust your introduction for perfect trading. After assessment, dissect your show and plan how you can perform and profit during the next trading session. With the help of a trading journal, you can have an obvious point of view on your general execution. This improves a forex trader's position.

What goes into an amazing trading journal:

Best sellers use a reasonable trading journal to advance their potential advantage. Much like a trading strategy, each forex representative will build their individual journal with information beneficial to their style. Here are subjects to consider recording in your trading journal:

Obvious:

1. Entry and leave date with forex pair
2. Trade execution and solicitation type
3. Length of the trades
4. Trade size and capital cut-off points
5. Results of the trade
6. Profits or setbacks from the trade
7. Market conditions of the day of trade
8. Long term market trends
9. Logic for segment or leave trade with threats
10. Ratio appraisals from advantages and productive trades

Execution:

1. Forex trading destinations and motivation
2. Trading perspective and execution
3. Strength and weaknesses from the trade
4. Thoughts and estimations toward the trade
5. Trading mix-ups with potential game plans

6.   Important and huge self-review request
7.   Future courses of action and updates
8.   Skills secured or capacities to be improved
9.   Emotional triggers when trading
10.   Performance level during the trade session

A powerful trader takes a gander at each particular trade, yet what's more, the development of their trading execution. Through a ground-breaking trading journal, forex representatives can surge the route towards an inexorably instructed and valuable trading calling. By misusing this mechanical assembly, you can gauge, examine and overhaul your trading method. You can totally screen your capacities, eager triggers and various pieces of trading you wish to evaluate and progress.

CHAPTER ONE
THE BASIC OF PERFORMING A TRADE

◆ ◆ ◆

In the event that you've investigated exchanging forex on the web and feel it's a potential chance to profit, you might ponder about the most ideal approach to consider going all in and figure out how to begin in forex trading.

It's essential to have a comprehension of the business sectors and techniques for forex trading with the goal that you can all the more successfully deal with your risk, make winning exchanges, and set yourself up for achievement in your new pursuit.

The Importance of Getting Educated

To exchange adequately, it's basic to get a forex instruction. You can discover a great deal of helpful data on forex here at The Balance. Invest some energy finding out about how forex trading functions, making forex exchanges, dynamic forex trading times, and overseeing risks, first of all.

As you may learn after some time, nothing beats understanding, and on the off chance that you need to get the hang of forex trading, background is the best educator. At the point when you first begin, you open a forex demo account and evaluate some demo trading. It will give you a decent specialized establishment on the mechanics of making forex exchanges and becoming accustomed to working with a particular trading stage.

An essential thing you may learn through involvement, that no measure of books or conversing with different merchants can instruct, is the benefit of shutting your exchange and escaping the market when your purpose behind getting into an exchange is discredited.

It is simple for dealers to figure the market will return around in their favor. You would be shocked what number of dealers fall prey to this snare and are astonished and grief stricken when the market just presses further against the heading of their unique exchange.

The well-known and horrendously evident articulation from John Maynard Keynes expresses, "The market can remain silly, longer than you can remain dissolvable." As it were, it does minimal great to state the market is acting nonsensically and that it will come around (which means toward your exchange) since extraordinary moves characterize capital markets in any case.

Utilize a Micro Forex Account

The problem of learning forex trading with a demo account alone is that you don't get the chance to encounter what it resembles to have your well-deserved cash on hold. Trading teachers regularly suggest that you open a miniaturized scale forex trading account or an account with a variable-exchange size that will enable you to make little exchanges.

Trading small will enable you to put some cash on hold, however, open yourself to exceptionally little misfortunes in the event that you commit errors or go into losing exchanges. This will encourage you unmistakably beyond what anything that you can peruse on a site, book, or forex trading gathering and gives an altogether new edge to whatever you'll learn while trading on a demo account.

Find out About the Currencies You Trade

To begin, you'll have to comprehend what you're trading. New merchants will in general hop in and start trading whatever appears as profitable. They generally will utilize high influence and exchange haphazardly in the two bearings, normally prompting loss of cash.

Understanding the monetary standards that you purchase and sell has a major effect. For instance, a money might skip upward after an enormous fall and urge unpracticed merchants to "attempt to get the base." The cash itself may have been falling because of awful business reports for different months. OK purchase something to that effect? Presumably not, and this is a case of why you have to know and comprehend what you purchase and sell.

Cash trading is extraordinary in light of the fact that you can utilize influence, and there are such huge numbers of various money sets to exchange. It doesn't mean, be that as it may, that you have to exchange them all. It's smarter to pick a pair that you understand and focus only on those. Having just a pair will make it simple to stay aware of financial news for the nations in question, and you'll have the option to get a feeling of the cadence of the monetary forms included.

After you've been trading with a little live account for some time and you know what you're doing, it's alright to store more cash and expand your measure of trading capital. Realizing what you're doing comes down to disposing of your unfortunate propensities, understanding the market and trading techniques, and dealing with your feelings. On the off chance that you can do that, you can be fruitful trading forex.

Benefit POTENTIAL

Numerous individuals like trading outside monetary forms on the remote trade (forex) showcase since it requires minimal measure of money to begin day trading, exchanges 24 hours per day (during the week) and offers a great deal of benefit potential because of the influence of forex merchants. The key question everybody has is, "How much cash would I be able to make trading forex in a day?" The accompanying situation demonstrates the potential, utilizing a risk controlled forex day trading methodology.

Forex Day Trading Risk Management

Each effective forex informal investor deals with their risk; it is one of, if not the, most pivotal components of continuous profits.

To begin, you should keep your risk on each exchange extremely little, and 1 percent or less is normal. This implies in the event that you have a $3,000 account, you shouldn't lose more than $30 on a solitary exchange (see Forex Position Sizing). That may appear to be little, however, losses do happen, and even a decent day-trading system will see series of misfortunes. Risk is overseen utilizing a stop misfortune request, which will be talked about in the Scenario segments beneath.

Forex Day Trading Strategy

While a methodology can possibly have numerous parts and can be broke down for benefit in different manners, a technique is regularly positioned dependent on its success rate and hazard/compensate proportion.

Your success rate speaks to the quantity of exchanges you win out a given all out number of exchanges. Let's assume you win 55 out of 100 exchanges, your success rate is 55 percent. While it isn't required, having a success rate over 50 percent is perfect for most informal investors, and 55 percent is adequate and achievable.

Hazard/remunerate connotes how much capital is being gambled to accomplish a specific benefit. On the off chance that a merchant loses 10 pips on losing exchanges however makes 15 on winning exchanges, she is making more on the victors than she's losing on washouts. This implies regardless of whether the broker just successes 50 percent of her exchanges, she will be beneficial. In this way, making more on winning exchanges is additionally a vital part for which numerous forex informal investors endeavor.

A higher success rate for exchanges implies greater adaptability with your hazard/compensate, and a high hazard/remunerate implies your success rate can be lower you'd even now be productive. For an increasingly careful exchange on win rate and hazard/compensate see: Day Trade Better Using Win Rate and Risk-Reward Ratios.

Situation: How Much Money Can I Make Forex Day Trading?

Expect a merchant has $5,000 in capital, and they have a not too bad win pace of 55 percent on their exchanges. They chance just 1 percent of their capital or $50 per exchange. This is practiced by utilizing a stop-misfortune request. For this situation, a stop-misfortune request is set 5 pips from the exchange passage cost, and an objective is put 8 pips away.

This implies the potential reward for each exchange is 1.6 occasions more prominent than the hazard (8/5). Keep in mind, you need victors to be greater than failures.

While trading a forex pair for two hours during a functioning time of day (see: Best Time of Day to Day Trade Forex) it's generally conceivable to make around five round turn exchanges (round turn incorporates section and leave) utilizing the above parameters. On the off chance that there are 20 trading days a month, the broker is making 100 exchanges, all things considered, in a month.

Forex specialists give influence up to 50:1 (more in certain nations). For this model, expect the merchant is utilizing 30:1 influence, as generally that is all that anyone could need influence for forex informal investors. Since the merchant has $5,000, and influence is 30:1, the dealer can take positions worth up to $150,000. Hazard is as yet dependent on the first $5,000; this keeps the hazard restricted to a little segment of the saved capital.

Forex dealers frequently don't charge a commission, but instead increment the spread between the offer and ask, along these lines making it increasingly hard to day exchange beneficially. ECN intermediaries offer an exceptionally little spread, making it simpler to exchange productively, however they commonly charge about $2.50 for each $100,000 exchanged ($5 round turn).

In case you're day trading a pair like the GBP/USD, you can hazard $50 on each exchange, and each pip of development is worth $10 with a standard parcel (100,000 units worth of cash). Along these lines you can take a place of one standard part with a 5-pip stop-misfortune request, which will keep the danger of misfortune to $50 on the exchange. That likewise implies a triumphant exchange is worth $80 (8 pips x $10).

This gauge can indicate how a lot of a forex informal investor could make in a month by executing 100 exchanges:

- 55 exchanges were gainful: 55 x $80 = $4,400
- 45 exchanges were washouts: 45 x ($50) = ($2,250)

Gross benefit is $4,400 - $2,250 = $2,150 if no commissions (win rate would almost certainly be lower however)

Net benefit is $2,150 - $500 = $1, 650 if utilizing a commission merchant (win rate would resemble be higher however)

Expecting a net benefit of $1,650, the arrival on the account for the month is 33 percent ($1,650/$5,000). This may appear to be extremely high, and it is a generally excellent return. See Refinements beneath to perceive how this arrival might be influenced.

Refinements

It won't generally be conceivable to discover five great day exchanges every day, particularly when the market is moving gradually for broadened timeframes.

Slippage is an inescapable piece of trading. It brings about a bigger misfortune than anticipated, in any event, when utilizing a stop misfortune request. It's basic in quick moving markets. To represent slippage in your potential benefits computation, decrease the net benefit by 10 percent (this is a high gauge for slippage, expecting you abstain from holding through major financial information discharges). This would decrease the net benefit potential created by your $5,000 trading cash-flow to $1,485 every month.

You can modify the situation above dependent on your run of the mill stop misfortune and target, capital, slippage, win rate, position size, and commission parameters.

The Final Word

This straightforward hazard controlled system shows that with a 55 percent win rate, and making more on champs than you lose on losing exchanges, it's conceivable to achieve returns north of 20 percent for every month with forex day trading. Most brokers shouldn't hope to make this much; while it sounds basic, in actuality, it's more troublesome.

All things considered, with a better than average win rate and hazard/remunerate proportion, a devoted forex informal investor with a good technique can make between 5 percent and 15 percent a month on account of influence. Likewise recollect you needn't bother with a lot of funding to begin; $500 to $1,000 is normally enough.

Digital forms of money

Digital money is a computerized cash worked with cryptographic conventions that make exchanges secure and hard to counterfeit.

THE HISTORY OF CYPTOCURRENCY

In 1983, the American cryptographer David Chaum imagined an unknown cryptographic electronic cash called ecash. Afterward, in 1995, he actualized it through Digicash, an early type of cryptographic electronic installments which required client programming so as to pull back notes from a bank and assign explicit encoded keys before it tends to be sent to a beneficiary. This enabled the advanced cash to be untraceable by the giving bank, the administration, or any outsider.

In 1998, Wei Dai distributed a portrayal of "b-cash", described as a mysterious, dispersed electronic money system. Shortly from there on, Nick Szabo depicted piece gold. Like bitcoin and different digital currencies that would tail it, bit gold (not to be mistaken for the later gold-based trade, BitGold) was portrayed as an electronic money framework which expected clients to finish a proof of work with arrangements being cryptographically assembled and distributed. A money framework dependent on a reusable confirmation of work was later made by Hal Finney who pursued crafted by Dai and Szabo.

The principal decentralized digital money, bitcoin, was made in 2009 by pseudonymous designer Satoshi Nakamoto. It utilized SHA-256, a cryptographic hash work, as its evidence of-work plot. In April 2011, Namecoin was made as an endeavor at shaping a decentralized DNS, which would make web oversight troublesome. Before long, in October 2011, Litecoin was discharged. It was the main fruitful digital currency to utilize scrypt as its hash work rather than SHA-256. Another eminent digital money, Peercoin was the first to utilize a proof-of-work/evidence of-stake cross breed.

On 6 August 2014, the UK reported its Treasury had been charged to do an investigation of cryptographic forms of money, and what job, assuming any, they can play in the UK economy. The examination was additionally to provide details regarding whether guideline ought to be considered

Step by step instructions to TRADE CRYPTO

There are approaches to exchange (purchase/sell) cryptocurrencies, for example, Bitcoin (BTC). Every way has its own upsides and drawbacks. As the cryptocurrency market keeps on developing, get to trading crypto will extend and wind up simpler. At last, what makes a difference most is utilizing a trade/online handle that you can trust.

Instructions to Trade Cryptocurrency

Fiat to Crypto Trading

In this way, you have some cash that you need to contribute. How are you going to go about it? The entryways which interface our reality to the crypto-universes are classified "trades." There are a ton of trades out there, be that as it may, before you put resources into one, there are sure things you have to pay special mind to. How about we consider this the "Trade Checklist."

- Validity: Before you even do anything, first ensure that the trade is accessible in your general vicinity. E.g. Coinbase, perhaps the biggest trade, isn't accessible in India and Indonesia. So before you do anything please check this.

- Reputation: Next thing that you have to check is the notoriety of the trade. Are individuals content with their administrations? Has it been hacked as of late? How secure is it? Have individuals grumbled about it? Twitter and Reddit are great hotspots for checking this.

- Exchange Rates: Up next we have the trade rates. Various trades have their own trade rates which may shift. Get your work done here and investigate 3 or 4 trades and their rates.

- Safety: Please consistently pick trades which need a type of ID check from you. Despite the fact that they may require significant investment, they are effectively multiple times more sheltered and secure than unknown trades. Toward the day's end, it is your well-deserved cash. You should make that additional move to keep it secure.

CONVERT DOLLARS TO CRYPTO, BLOCKCHAIN

Store your crypto before changing over it

In the event that you need to change over digital money to money, you should make a wallet first to get your crypto. It is commonly important to claim one single wallet for every digital money yet some easy to use wallets like Exodus.io enable you to oversee different resources through one single interface.

Understand that the Bitcoin or Ethereum blockchains are systems, similar to the web is itself. The wallets we are going to cover underneath are customers enabling access to these systems. As one of the result of this, you may get to a blockchain through various focuses, some are more secure or easy to use than others:

- Hot wallets
- Software wallets
- Cold wallets

The standard number one, regardless of the wallet you have chosen to utilize, is to NEVER impart your private keys to anybody. They are what might be compared to the PIN of your plastic. Anybody realizing your private keys approach your assets without your assent.

Get crypto in hot wallets

The term 'hot' wallet alludes to a digital currency wallet that is associated with the web as it were. The most widely recognized hot wallets allude to the wallets you claim on digital currency trades.

In any case, programming wallets, that are programming introduced on your PC, are associated with the web as well and can be considered as hot wallets too.

1. Your wallet on a cryptographic money trade

On the off chance that you purchase a digital currency just because, you may need to experience a cryptographic money trade. You should make a record and check it through a KYC. Every one of these stages have preferences and disadvantages, others exist yet instances of the most dependable are Bitstamp.net, Bitpanda.com, Coinbase.com and child on.

Every one of the sites above will enable you to purchase digital forms of money with your VISA card or because of a bank move or other installment strategies. These sites are the ones enabling you to change over Bitcoin to USD or to EUR too, and to cashout the sum in USD or EUR to your financial balance.

On the off chance that you gave your trade wallet address to the individual sending you cash, you can straightforwardly bounce to the believer crypto to money section toward the finish of this post. Note in any case, that you ought not make a propensity for utilizing your trade wallet methodically for exchanges. Your trade wallet is as protected as the trade is and in a continually changing condition like the crypto-world is, that suggests direct legitimate, specialized and security dangers for your assets. Kindly consider the accompanying putting away alternatives as well.

2. Programming wallets

Before downloading a wallet, it is essential to know which digital money you need to get or purchase and move to your wallet. On the off chance that you need to change over Bitcoin to USD, you will require a bitcoin wallet, on the off chance that you need to change over Ethereum, you are going to require an Ethereum wallet first. Note that trades are furnishing you with a few wallets (BTC, ETH, LTC, BCH and so forth.) for you opening as well (less complex, yet once more, not as protected):

• Bitcoin wallets: Electrum is probably the least complex alternative out there. Different alternatives like Exodus.io enable you to see adjusts for different resources claimed on the blockchain like Ethereum yet not just. For a progressively exhaustive rundown of Bitcoin wallets, it would be ideal if you visit the bitcoin.org site.

- Ethereum wallets: Websites like mycrypto.com and myetherwallet.com allow you to make an Ethereum wallet and access the Ethereum blockchain in that capacity. These are the least difficult and most secure 'hot' wallets alternatives with Metamask.io. The last can flaunt a helpful program module for an extra effectiveness of utilization. Ethereum can be sent on these wallets just as ERC20 tokens gave on the Ethereum blockchain.

- Other wallets: For some other crypto resources than Ethereum or Bitcoin, kindly allude to the proper documentation on the site of the task being referred to. Before purchasing any sort of crypto, it is significant that you know precisely what sort of wallet is operational for the crypto resource you are purchasing.

'Hot' capacity is known to be simple of utilization and to be a pleasant prologue to the blockchain innovation yet it ought not be utilized to store what you think about a high measure of cash on the since quite a while ago run. On the off chance that you intend to possess cryptographic forms of money on the since a long time ago run, you should purchase a cool wallet.

Get crypto on chilly wallets

1. Equipment wallets

'Cold' wallets go under the type of USB blaze drives and are the most secure approach to store and move digital currencies. While they do get to the blockchain on the web, your assets are as sheltered as your USB blaze drive seems to be. With the dynamic appropriation of blockchain and digital currencies, a few organizations have made their cool wallets, the two fundamental ones right now are:

- Ledger
- Trezor

Different names are well respectable and worth your consideration as well yet we will consider these two as the principle ones as they have been doing business for quite a long time, before any other person, which is an or more with regards to issues like putting away cash.

2. Paper wallets

A paper wallet comprises of a print or a manually written note of your private keys. All things considered your assets are as sheltered as the paper your private keys are composed on is. Remember, in any case, that your private keys ought not be reordered for ideal wellbeing of your assets with the goal that this valuable data doesn't remain in your PC's clipboard. The equivalent goes with printing it…

In the event that you compose your private keys straightforwardly from your screen, ensure you duplicate the location right (they are in every case extremely long and confounding) and that your PC is absolutely infection free.

This is the reason, consistently, it is principal that you keep the authority over your private keys. While you can change over crypto to money in a split second on trades, on the off chance that you store digital money on them, they are responsible for your private keys and you are not, with all the guarantee hazards that suggests.

Digital currency move to your wallet

Since you have picked the most helpful wallet for your utilization, you can get digital currency. Keep in mind it is significant you give a Bitcoin wallet address on the off chance that you are going to get Bitcoins or an Ethereum wallet address in the event that you are going to be sent Ethereum or ERC20 tokens.

The equivalent is valid with some other digital currencies: consistently watch that the wallet address you are conveying can get the given cryptographic money. This is essential to consider as there are more than 1,500 out there and tallying. A few names can be mistaking for individuals entering the cryptographic money world.

Convert digital currency into money in your financial balance

At the hour of this article, no bank will change over digital money into money. A few tasks are attempting to offer comparable administrations yet some are exceptionally later and others are still being developed stage. The least expensive alternative is to change over your cryptographic money on a trade site for USD, EUR or your nearby cash.

For the American dollars and the euro, you can utilize the trades recorded previously.

For every one of them, you should experience a confirmation procedure that will expect you to send an ID record and a service bill. By and large, your ledger should be checked also by playing out a test exchange from it.

Digital currency store to the trade: A wallet-to-wallet move

When you made a record on your favored trade site, you will approach a few wallet addresses. The wallets on the trade are yours as well, yet they will enable you to change over your cryptographic money into money and after that move it to your financial balance. Presently you simply need to send your cryptographic money from your present wallet to the wallet you possess on the trade site:

- Depending on your wallet, discover the best approach to send the digital money put away on it by squeezing a 'send' button. Given it is one of the center component of your wallet, it ought to be anything but difficult to detect regardless of the wallet utilized.

- At this point, you will be required to enter a goal address. Incredible news! The goal address is the location of the wallet you possess on the trade site you opened your account on. Be mindful so as to give the correct location for the correct resource. A Bitcoin address for a Bitcoin exchange, an Ethereum address for an Ethereum exchange and so on.

- Paste it in the goal address field of the wallet putting away your digital money right now.

- Triple check the goal address you reordered in your wallet of birthplace is a similar location shown in your trade account.

- Press send. The exchange ought not take in excess of a couple of moments. It can take longer now and then however you can check the status of your exchange by checking it on the blockchain itself with your exchange ID. (Blockchain.com for Bitcoin and Etherscan.io for Ethereum and ERC20 tokens)

Convert digital currency to money

Presently you ought to have the sum you sent to the trade showing up in your trade cryptographic money account balance. Most trades will send you an email store affirmation as well.

While it could simply be viewed as a transformation from cryptographic money to money, you are currently going to sell your digital money and purchase money with it as you would do at the air terminal money evolving work area.

In the event that you need to change over Bitcoin to USD, you should discover the BTC/USD advertise in your trade site. In the event that you need to change over Ethereum to EUR, you should discover the ETH/EUR showcase. Same goes with LTC, BCH, ETC, DASH, XMR against GBP, HKD, CAD, AUD, JPY and so forth. Discover the market that suits your need.

Convert cryptographic money to money on Bitstamp.net. Go to Tradeview.

Convert cryptographic money to money on Bitstamp.net. Pick your market.

When you are available page, as you would prefer not to exchange and need to change over your digital money immediately, you will sell it at market cost or 'market sell' it. To sell the fastest conceivable, select the value that is arranged at the highest point of the 'Offer' segment (hued green in the beneath model).

Offers are alluding to what purchasers of the digital currency you are selling are prepared to pay to get it. It is normally lower than the 'Ask' section which speaks to what dealers (you all things considered) are soliciting to get free from it.

Convert digital currency to money on Bitstamp.net. Sell Bitcoin to purchase USD.

In the event that you chose an offer cost for the perfect measure of digital money you are selling (check the segment 'Sum' on the left of the 'Offer' segment to ensure there is sufficient Bitcoin purchasing offer at the value you are selling), your sell request should take seconds to finish.

When this is done, a parity in the nearby money you sold your cryptographic money for will show up. You have recently changed over digital currency into money.

For the previously mentioned monetary standards there will be sufficient liquidity yet be cautious in attempting to sell less referred to monetary standards as there probably won't be purchasers to take care of your sell orders. On the off chance that you pursue this guide, you ought not have this issue yet this is continually an interesting point.

Cashout from the trade to your financial balance

On the off chance that and just if your trade record is confirmed and your KYC procedure has come about fruitful, you can demand a bank move cash out of the money parity showing up in your trade account to your ledger tolerating a similar cash (check conditions with your trade site).

The assets should arrive at your account in the five after business days. In the event that your trade site confirmed your VISA card, the money will be come back to the account connected with the checked VISA card.

Change FROM BITCOIN TO UNITED DOLLARS

The Markets Insider money adding machine offers a cash transformation from Bitcoin to United States dollar inside seconds. Vacationers in Bitcoin can make changes at the present conversion scale. The money adding machine gives a perfect apparatus to financial specialists putting resources into universal stock trades with various monetary forms.

Transformation from Bitcoin to United States dollar should be possible at current rates just as at recorded rates – to do this, select the ideal conversion scale date. The present date is set naturally. Furthermore, the money adding machine demonstrates the end pace of the earlier day just as the most elevated and least paces of the transformation Bitcoin - United States dollar. The outcomes are shown in an unmistakably masterminded table. Notwithstanding the Bitcoin - United States dollar rate, the Markets Insider cash adding machine likewise offers other trade rates for around 160 global monetary standards.

BITCOIN - UNITED STATES DOLLAR CURRENCY CALCULATOR

You have at present chosen the base money Bitcoin and the objective cash United States dollar with a measure of 1 Bitcoin. In the menu, you can choose the ideal trade paces of around 160 global monetary forms from the two accounts. Also, the money number cruncher enables you to compute chronicled trade rates notwithstanding the present rate. The outcomes are shown in a table with the end pace of the earlier day, the opening rate just as the least and most noteworthy paces of the individual date

FOREX, STOCKS, OPTIONS

Choices Or Forex Trading?

Two of the prevalent markets accessible to brokers in the money related world are investment opportunities and cash trading on the forex markets. The theme frequently comes up which one is better? They are both altogether different creatures and a dealer should know about those distinctions to ensure they are exchanging the market that best accommodates their trading style and benefit objectives.

Initially, how about we characterize each market. When trading alternatives you can control both the upside and drawback development in a stock, ETF, or Index item. Utilizing a call choice will give you control of the upside development in a stock, while a put choice will give you control of the drawback development in a stock. These are items that enable the retail dealer to control 100 portions of stock for a small amount of the cost when contrasted with purchasing the portions of stock by and large.

When trading in the forex markets, a broker is hoping to benefit from changing money trade rates. Money markets exchange sets. A dealer is wagering on changing trade rates between the two monetary forms that make up that pair. For instance, when exchanging the EUR/USD the broker is making wagers on the changing conversion scale between the Euro and the U.S. Dollar. Forex trading is additionally an incredible route for the retail dealer to engage in the business sectors with a littler account size because of the influence that these items offer.

Geniuses and Cons Of Options Trading

While these are both possibly entirely beneficial markets for dealers to take a gander at, the two of them have their upsides and downsides. How about we stroll through a portion of those upsides and downsides of the alternatives advertises first. Choices are incredible in light of the fact that they are profoundly directed items that exchange on incorporated trades. When going into a situation with choices, you have the genuine feelings of serenity realizing that these agreements are sponsored by a trade which means you won't need to stress over the individual on the opposite side of the exchange not satisfying their side of the arrangement. You likewise realize that the value that you are seeing when going into an exchange on your merchant stage is a similar value that is cited on an alternate stage. This is imperative to call attention to as you will see the distinction when we get to the forex markets. Choices are additionally the main budgetary item that offer you the chance to make cash in up, down, and sideways moving conditions. Every other item require the business sectors to go up or down to profit.

On the drawback, alternatives are just exchanged from 9:30-4:00 New York time. For brokers in various pieces of the world this can be an issue contingent upon the time change. For a merchant in Australia, exchanging the U.S. session can be an issue considering the time change. Alternatives additionally have time rot which means they are squandering resources. The more you hold them the less worth they have, which means you should be spot on bearing as well as need the stock to move quick enough.

Geniuses and Cons Of Forex Trading

When taking a gander at the Forex markets, there are additionally advantages and disadvantages. How about we take a gander at the advantages first. Forex markets enable a merchant to begin with as meager as a couple of hundred dollars, which is incredible for the little retail dealer. This can likewise enable a dealer to effortlessly enhance their portfolio by having the option to see more markets. These business sectors are open 24 hours every day which is an incredible component for merchants all around the globe. Given how dynamic the world markets are nowadays, approaching the business sectors 24 hours daily can be an enormous bit of leeway. This entrance can enable a dealer to respond to news snappier than most different markets. Forex showcases additionally offer distinctive agreement sizes. Brokers can exchange full, smaller than usual and miniaturized scale little size shares. This enables the forex dealer to oversee chance simpler than different markets.

On the drawback, forex markets can likewise be dubious in light of the fact that they aren't exceptionally directed. There is no brought together trade where these items exchange like numerous different markets. This implies a dealer's prosperity or disappointment could rely upon the costs being cited to them by their specialist. As a rule the forex intermediary is taking the opposite side of your exchanges causing an irreconcilable circumstance. This element alone can frighten numerous dealers off from the forex markets. Forex markets being open 24 hours daily can be seen as an advantage, however, can likewise be seen as an issue. Realizing that these business sectors are open 24 hours daily can prompt over trading.

Choice – Conclusion

- The stock buy is a customary speculation item where the financial specialist puts resources into an organization offers and anticipate returns as profit and capital appreciation.
- On the other hand, alternatives are a cutting edge subsidiary item where the dealers gain/misfortune dependent on the development of a stock value an incentive later on time by paying a little premium add up to the essayist of choice as opposed to contributing the sum equivalent to share esteem.

- So to finish up, Stock and Option are both significant portfolio devices for a speculator where stocks are useful for long haul venture reason and choices are best who appreciate the adaptability and diminish the hazard by supporting.

Choices Vs. Forex: The Final Verdict?

So which one is a superior item for trading, choices or forex? The response to this inquiry in many cases boils down to individual inclination. In my own trading, I lean toward the managed markets in the alternatives space. In the same way as other different dealers, I don't need my agent to take the opposite side of my exchanges. I need to battle a reasonable battle. The 24 hours get to that the forex markets offer is an issue for me. I like the capacity to put my alternatives exchanges during the U.S. securities exchange hours and after that not need to stress over them again until the following morning. Having the option to close down after the market closes is a major factor in me picking the choices showcase. As should be obvious my decision in picking the alternatives advertise truly boils down to individual inclination. Shows improvement over the other? There is anything but a general response to that question. A dealer needs to assess their own objectives, considering their hazard resistance and day by day timetable to figure out which markets are best for their needs.

CHAPTER TWO

CANDLESTICK STRATEGY

◆ ◆ ◆

Candle graphs are a specialized apparatus that pack information for various time allotments into single value bars. This makes them more valuable than customary open-high, low-close bars (OHLC) or basic lines that draw an obvious conclusion of shutting costs. Candles manufacture designs that anticipate value heading once finished. Legitimate shading coding adds profundity to this vivid specialized device, which goes back to eighteenth century Japanese rice dealers.

Steve Nison brought candle examples toward the Western world in his prevalent 1991 book, "Japanese Candlestick Charting Techniques." Many merchants would now be able to recognize many these arrangements, which have vivid names like bearish foreboding shadow spread, evening star and three dark crows. Likewise, single bar examples including the doji and mallet have been joined into many long-and short-side trading techniques.

Candle Pattern Reliability

Not all candle examples work similarly well. Their immense ubiquity has brought down dependability since they've been deconstructed by flexible investments and their calculations. These well-subsidized players depend on lightning-speed execution to exchange against retail financial specialists and customary store directors who execute specialized investigation procedures found in famous writings. At the end of the day, flexible investments managers use programming to trap members searching for high-chances bullish or bearish results. Be that as it may, dependable examples keep on showing up, taking into account short-and long haul benefit openings.

Here are five candle designs that perform especially well as forerunners of value course and energy. Every work inside the setting of encompassing value bars in anticipating higher or lower costs. They are additionally time touchy in two different ways. In the first place, they just work inside the confinements of the graph being checked on, regardless of whether intraday, every day, week after week or month to month. Second, their intensity diminishes quickly three to five bars after the example has finished.

Top 5 Candlestick Patterns

This investigation depends on crafted by Thomas Bulkowski, who assembled execution rankings for candle designs in his 2008 book, "Reference book of Candlestick Charts." He offers measurements for two sorts of expected example results: reversal and continuation. Candle inversion examples anticipate an adjustment in value bearing, while continuation examples foresee an augmentation in the present value course.

In the accompanying models, the empty white candle means an end print higher than the opening print, while the dark candle signifies an end print lower than the opening print.

Three Line Strike

The bullish three line strike inversion example cuts out three dark candles inside a downtrend. Each bar posts a lower low and closes close the intrabar low. The fourth bar opens even lower however inverts in a wide-go outside bar that closes over the high of the primary flame in the arrangement. The opening print likewise denotes the low of the fourth bar. As indicated by Bulkowski, this inversion predicts more significant expenses with an 84% exactness rate.

Two Black Gapping

The bearish two dark gapping continuation example shows up after a striking top in an upswing, with a hole down that yields two dark bars posting lower lows. This example predicts that the decay will keep on night lower lows, maybe setting off a more extensive scale downtrend. As indicated by Bulkowski, this example predicts lower costs with a 68% precision rate.

Three Black Crows

The bearish three dark crows inversion example begins at or close to the high of an upswing, with three dark bars posting lower lows that nearby close intrabar lows. This example predicts that the decay will keep on night lower lows, maybe setting off a more extensive scale downtrend. The most bearish form begins at another high (point An on the graph) since it traps purchasers entering force plays. As indicated by Bulkowski, this example predicts lower costs with a 78% exactness rate.

Night Star

The bearish night star inversion example begins with a tall white bar that conveys an upswing to another high. The market holes higher on the following bar, yet crisp purchasers neglect to show up, yielding a tight range candle. A hole down on the third bar finishes the example, which predicts that the decrease will keep on night lower lows, maybe setting off a more extensive scale downtrend. As indicated by Bulkowski, this example predicts lower costs with a 72% precision rate.

Surrendered Baby

The bullish surrendered child inversion example shows up at the low of a downtrend, after a progression of dark candles print lower lows. The market holes lower on the following bar, however new dealers neglect to show up, yielding a limited range doji candle with opening and shutting prints at a similar cost. A bullish hole on the third bar finishes the example, which predicts that the recuperation will keep on night higher highs, maybe setting off a more extensive scale upswing. As indicated by Bulkowski, this example predicts more significant expenses with a 70% exactness rate.

The Bottom Line

Candle examples catch the consideration of market players, yet numerous inversion and continuation sign transmitted by these examples don't work dependably in the cutting edge electronic condition. Luckily, measurements by Thomas Bulkowski show irregular exactness for a restricted determination of these examples, offering merchants significant purchase and sell signals.

Putting the experiences picked up from seeing candle examples to utilize and putting resources into an advantage dependent on them would require a money market fund. To spare some examination time, Investopedia has assembled a rundown of the best online brokers so you can locate the correct intermediary for your venture needs.

Candle PATTERNS, SINGLE AND MULTIPLE

Another sort of specialized examination that we will cover is essential single candle designs, as they are anything but difficult to distinguish and translate.

Turning Top

A turning top has two long equivalent length shadows with a little body and normally flag an inversion when they happen during a pattern. The purpose for the inversion is that it indicates uncertainty among purchasers and dealers, and that neither of them can close a lot higher or lower than the opening.

Most dealers utilize the procedure of going long a money pair if a turning top happens during a downtrend and shorting a couple on the off chance that it happens during a downtrend.

Maruboza

A Maruboza is the point at which a candle structures with a long body and practically zero shadow. This sign solid development one way, which will probably proceed with development toward that path sooner rather than later. In the bullish Maruboza case, the opening cost is equivalent to the low and the end cost is equivalent to the high. With a bearish Maruboza the opening cost is the high and the end is the low.

Doji

A doji is where the opening cost is nearly precisely the same as the opening cost, with long shadows a single way or both. What this can flag is uncertainty among purchasers and dealers. In the event that these happen at the top or base of a pattern it can flag an inversion as it demonstrates an easing back of energy.

Sledge

The sledge outline example is a Japanese candle that has a little body with a short to no shadow over the body with a long shadow on the base. At the point when this candle happens at the base of a pattern, it can flag for an inversion.

Hanging Man

The hanging man candle example has precisely the same candle as the sledge however has diverse value activity before it, so it signals for an inversion downwards.

Transformed Hammer

The transformed sledge is a candle like the mallet and hanging man designs in that it can flag an inversion. With a transformed mallet, a little bullish candle body structures with a long shadow on top, and happens during a downtrend.

The explanation this flag a conceivable inversion is a direct result of a powerlessness of the bears to constrain the cost beneath the nearby after a solid exertion by the bulls. The deficiency of merchants is a sign for a change towards upward energy.

Falling star

The falling star is like the transformed mallet yet happens during an upswing and can flag an inversion downwards. The candle for a meteorite is a little bearish body with a long shadow on top.

The purpose for the inversion in quality is that the confirms reinforced the bulls after a solid push by the bulls. At the point when this happens during an upswing it connotes an adjustment in energy downwards.

Graph ANATOMY

A short prologue to Forex diagramming:

The accompanying article will give you an extremely essential presentation into the universe of Forex graphing. It is intended for individuals with no earlier graphing learning and furthermore for the individuals who might want a snappy reference manage or an update on the essential diagram types that we use in Forex. Since perusing graphs is the premise of what we do here at Learn To Trade The Market, we have to begin from a strong establishment and get the essentials of diagramming of the way. This material will give you the essential data you should bode well out of the various data on my site just as my Forex trading course. So how about we begin with your first Forex trading exercise...

The Line Chart:

Regardless of whether you have no past understanding or information of trading the business sectors you have most likely observed a line graph of cost on the evening news or in a reading material sooner or later. A line graph gives you a decent depiction of market heading by associating a line starting with one shutting value then onto the next (You can set them to show open, high or low costs as well, yet the end cost is generally prevalent). Most dealers put a more noteworthy accentuation on the end cost of any trading instrument, so the line outline can give you an important perspective on market development over some undefined time frame.

Here is what a line outline resembles:

As should be obvious from the line outline over, the ongoing pattern daily for EUR/USD is up albeit at present is amidst a descending rectification and has been extend bound generally this year. Zooming out and taking a gander at a day by day or week after week line outline can give you a smart thought of overwhelming pattern heading. It is anything but difficult to stall out taking a gander at 1hour or lower diagrams which innately have a great deal of "clamor" or futile data, line outlines can give you a decent longer term point of view to help keep you grounded. My Forex trading course primarily utilizes candle outlines which are the most prominent diagrams and the ones you will experience the most. We will cover candle outlines after bar diagrams beneath...

The Bar Chart:

A bar graph demonstrates the end cost just as the open, high, and low cost for the timespan you are taking a gander at. The highest point of the vertical bar demonstrates the most significant expense paid during that timespan while the base of the bar shows the least value paid during that timeframe. The whole length of the bar through and through in this manner demonstrates the scope of cost over the timespan you are taking a gander at. You will see that every individual bar likewise has a hash on the left and a hash on the correct side of the bar. The hash on the left side demonstrates the opening value during that timespan, the hash on the correct side shows the end cost for that timeframe.

NOTE: A bar is just one portion of time, regardless of whether it is one day, multi week, or 60 minutes. Bar outlines are likewise called "OHLC" diagrams, since they show the Open, the High, the Low, and the Close for that specific cash.

Here's a case of a value bar:

Open: The little even line on the left is the opening cost

High: The highest point of the vertical line characterizes the most significant expense of the timespan

Low: The base of the vertical line characterizes the least cost of the timespan

Close: The little level line on the privilege is the end cost

Here is a similar diagram utilized in the line outline clarification however in bar graph structure:

Candle outlines:

Candle diagrams demonstrate a similar data as a bar outline yet in a graphical configuration that is increasingly fun and valuable to take a gander at.

Candle outlines demonstrate the high and low of the given timeframe similarly as bar diagrams do, with a vertical line. The top vertical line is known as the upper shadow while the base vertical line is known as the lower shadow; you may likewise observe the upper and lower shadows alluded to as "wicks". The primary distinction lies in how candle graphs show the opening and shutting cost. The enormous square in the center of the candle demonstrates the range between the opening and shutting cost. Generally this square is known as the "genuine body". By and large if the genuine body is filled in, or strong/darker in shading the money shut lower than it opened, and if the genuine body is left unfilled, or typically simply white/light hued, the cash shut higher than it opened. So if the genuine body is strong in shading than the highest point of the genuine body demonstrates the open cost and the base of the genuine body shows the end cost. In the event that the genuine body is unfilled or generally white, the highest point of the genuine body demonstrates the end cost and the base shows the open cost. This will all move toward becoming more clear with a representation...

Here's a case of a candle value bar:

Here is a similar outline utilized in the line and bar graph clarifications yet in candle diagram structure:

By changing the shading on your candle diagram it can make it simpler and all the more engaging take a gander at, red and blue are regularly utilized as substitute hues, notwithstanding, I favor highly contrasting and you will see most graphs on my site in highly contrasting. Here we have substituted blue for the white candle and red for the dark candle. At the end of the day, blue is a bull flame (which means the nearby was higher than the open), and red is a bear light (which means the nearby was lower than the open).

Candles are presumably the most mainstream of every one of the three graph structures among merchants since they are outwardly simpler on your eyes and they enable you to all the more effectively catch flag and patterns. Candles make finding out about value activity a lot simpler and all the more unwinding on the eye and the mind.

ABCD PATTERN

The ABCD is a fundamental consonant example. Every single other example get from it. The example comprises of 3 value swings. The lines AB and CD are classified "legs", while the line BC is alluded to as a redress or a retracement. Stomach muscle and CD will in general have roughly a similar size.

A bullish ABCD example pursues a downtrend and implies that an inversion to the upside is likely. A bearish ABCD example is shaped after an upturn and sign a potential bearish inversion at a specific level. The guidelines for trading in bullish and bearish ABCD examples are the equivalent, you will simply need to consider the course of the example you exchange and the development of the market it predicts.

There are a few sorts of ABCD design (all the 3 examples at the image are bullish).

In the great one, the point C ought to be at 61.8%-78.6% of AB (Use Fibonacci retracement instrument on AB: the point C ought to be near 61.8%). The point D, in its turn, ought to be at the 127.2%-161.8% Fibonacci development of BC.

Notice that a 61.8% retracement at the point C will in general outcome in the 161.8% projection of BC, while a 78.6% retracement at the C point will prompt the 127% projection.

There is likewise the alleged AB=CD design. Here CD has the very same length as AB. Likewise, it sets aside the market the equivalent effort to venture out from A to B as from C to D. As a Result, AB and CD have a similar edge. This kind of ABCD example is seen regularly and is prominent among brokers.

The third kind is when CD is the 127.2%-161.8% augmentation of AB. Cd can be even multiple times (or increasingly) greater than AB. There really are a few signs that can indicate that CD will be any longer than AB. They are a hole after point C or huge candles close to point C.

The most effective method to exchange ABCD design

The key thing you ought to recall is that you can enter the exchange simply after the value arrived at the point D.

Concentrate the diagram taking a gander at the value's highs and lows. It might be useful to utilize ZigZag pointer (Insert – Indicators – Custom – ZigZag) that denotes the diagram's swings.

Watch the cost as it structures AB and BC. In a bullish ABCD, C must be lower than An and ought to be the halfway high after the low at B. Point D must be a new low underneath B.

At the point when the market lands at a point, where D might be arranged, don't hurry into an exchange. Utilize a few methods to ensure that the value switched up (or down if it's a bearish ABCD). The best situation is an inversion candle design. A purchase request might be set at or over the high of the light at point D.

Take benefit levels

Here are the objective levels for trading the ABCD design.

TP1: 38.2% retracement of AD

TP2: 61.8% retracement of AD

TP3: point A

We prescribe utilizing these levels together with help and obstruction you recognize at the graph utilizing different apparatuses of specialized investigation. Remember to examine senior time allotments when you chase for help and obstruction levels.

On the off chance that the value moved to TP1 quick, the chances are that it will proceed towards TP2. In actuality, if the cost is delayed to get to TP1, this may imply that it will be the main TP level you'll get.

There are numerous situations when the market turned around after AC=CD example going past point A.

Concerning Stop Loss, there are no uncommon proposals. You can place a Stop Loss in accordance with your hazard the executives rules.

HOW WE TRADE IN FOREX MARKET

One of a kind part of this worldwide market is that there is no focal commercial center for outside trade. Or maybe, money exchanging is directed electronically over-the-counter (OTC), which implies that all exchanges happen through PC organizes between brokers the world over, as opposed to on one unified trade. The market is open 24 hours per day, five and a half days seven days, and monetary forms are exchanged worldwide the major budgetary focuses of London, New York, Tokyo, Zurich, Frankfurt, Hong Kong, Singapore, Paris and Sydney - crosswise over pretty much every time zone. This implies when the trading day in the U.S. closes, the Forex market starts once again in Tokyo and Hong Kong. In that capacity, the Forex market can be incredibly dynamic whenever of the day, with value statements evolving continually.

Spot Market and the Forwards and Futures Markets

There are three different ways that establishments, partnerships, and people exchange Forex: the spot advertise, the advances showcase, and the fates showcase. The Forex market has consistently been the biggest market since it is the "basic" genuine resource that all other markets depend on. Before, the prospects market was the most well-known setting for merchants since it was accessible to singular financial specialists for a more drawn out period. Notwithstanding, with the coming of electronic exchanging and various Forex handles, the spot market has seen a colossal flood in movement and now outperforms the prospects showcase as the favored exchanging market for individual financial specialists and theorists. At the point when individuals allude to the Forex showcase, they for the most part are alluding to the spot advertise. The advances and prospects markets will in general be progressively famous with organizations that need to fence their outside trade dangers out to a particular date later on.

All the more explicitly, the spot market is the place monetary forms are purchased and sold by the present cost. That value, controlled by organic market, is an impression of numerous things, including current financing costs, monetary execution, assumption towards continuous political circumstances (both locally and universally), just as the view of things to come execution of one cash against another. At the point when an arrangement is concluded, this is known as a "spot bargain." It is a respective exchange by which one gathering conveys a settled upon money add up to the counterparty and gets a predetermined measure of another cash at the settled upon swapping scale esteem. After a position is shut, the repayment is in real money. In spite of the fact that the spot market is generally known as one that manages exchanges in the present (instead of things to come), these exchanges take two days for settlement.

Dissimilar to the spot advertise, the advances and fates markets don't exchange genuine monetary forms. Rather, they bargain in agreements that speak to cases to a specific cash type, a particular value for every unit, and a future date for repayment.

In the advances advertise, contracts are purchased and sold OTC between two gatherings, who decide the conditions of the understanding between themselves.

In the prospects showcase, fates agreements are purchased and sold dependent on a standard size and settlement date on open items markets, for example, the Chicago Mercantile Exchange. In the U.S., the National Futures Association manages the prospects showcase. Fates agreements have explicit subtleties, including the quantity of units being exchanged, conveyance and settlement dates, and least value increases that can't be tweaked. The trade goes about as a partner to the dealer, giving freedom and settlement.

The two sorts of agreements are official and are normally made with money for the trade being referred to upon expiry, despite the fact that agreements can likewise be purchased and sold before they lapse. The advances and fates markets can offer security against hazard when exchanging monetary forms. Generally, enormous worldwide companies utilize these business sectors to support against future swapping scale variances, yet theorists participate in these business sectors also.

Note that you'll see the terms: FX, Forex, remote trade market and money showcase. These terms are synonymous, and all allude to the Forex showcase.

Forex as a Hedge

Organizations working together in remote nations are in danger because of changes in cash esteems when they purchase or sell products and enterprises outside of their residential market. Outside trade markets give an approach to fence money chance by fixing a rate at which the exchange will be finished.

To achieve this, a dealer can purchase or sell monetary forms in the forward or swap showcases ahead of time, which secures a conversion scale. For instance, envision that an organization intends to sell U.S.- made blenders in Europe when the swapping scale between the euro and the dollar (EUR/USD) is €1 to $1 at equality.

The blender costs $100 to make, and the U.S. firm intends to sell it for €150 – which is aggressive with different blenders that were made in Europe. On the off chance that this arrangement is effective, the organization will make $50 in benefit in light of the fact that the EUR/USD conversion scale is even. Lamentably, the USD starts to ascend in worth versus the euro until the EUR/USD conversion scale is .80, which means it currently costs $0.80 to purchase €1.00.

The issue the organization appearances is that it, while regardless it costs $100 to make the blender, the organization can just sell the item at the aggressive cost of €150, which when made an interpretation of once again into dollars is just $120 (€150 X .80 = $120). A more grounded dollar brought about a much smaller profit than anticipated.

The blender organization could have diminished this hazard by shorting the euro and purchasing the USD when they were at equality. That way, if the dollar rose in worth, the benefits from the exchange would counterbalance the decreased benefit from the clearance of blenders. In the event that the USD fell in worth, the more great conversion scale will build the benefit from the clearance of blenders, which balances the misfortunes in the exchange.

Supporting of this sort should be possible in the cash prospects advertise. The preferred position for the dealer is that fates agreements are institutionalized and cleared by a focal power. Notwithstanding, cash prospects might be less fluid than the forward business sectors, which are decentralized and exist inside the interbank framework all through the world.

Forex as Speculation

Components like loan costs, exchange streams, the travel industry, monetary quality, and geopolitical hazard influence organic market for monetary forms, which makes day by day instability in the Forex markets. An open door exists to benefit from changes that may increment or diminish one money's worth contrasted with another. A gauge that one money will debilitate is basically equivalent to accepting that the other cash in the pair will reinforce in light of the fact that monetary standards are exchanged as sets.

Envision a merchant who expects financing costs to ascend in the U.S. contrasted with Australia while the swapping scale between the two monetary forms (AUD/USD) is .71 (it takes USD .71 to purchase AUD 1.00). The dealer accepts higher loan fees in the U.S. will build interest for USD, and hence, the AUD/USD swapping scale will fall since it will require less, more grounded USD to purchase an AUD.

Accept that the broker is right and loan fees rise, which diminishes the AUD/USD conversion scale to .50. This implies it requires USD .50 to purchase AUD 1.00. In the event that the financial specialist had shorted the AUD and went long the USD, the individual would have benefitted from the adjustment in worth.

Cash as an Asset Class

There are two unmistakable highlights to monetary standards as an advantage class:

- You can procure the loan cost differential between two monetary forms.
- You can benefit from changes in the swapping scale.

A financial specialist can benefit from the distinction between two loan fees in two unique economies by purchasing the money with the higher loan cost and shorting the cash with the lower loan cost. Preceding the 2008 monetary emergency, it was normal to short the Japanese yen (JPY) and purchase British pounds (GBP) on the grounds that the loan fee differential was huge. This procedure is some of the time alluded to as a "convey exchange."

Why We Can Trade Currencies

Cash exchanging was hard for individual financial specialists before the web. Most cash brokers were huge worldwide partnerships, flexible investments or high-total assets people in light of the fact that Forex exchanging required a ton of capital. With assistance from the web, a retail market went for individual merchants has risen, giving simple access to the outside trade markets, either through the banks themselves or representatives making an auxiliary market. Most online representatives or sellers offer high influence to singular merchants who can control a huge exchange with a little account balance.

Forex Trading Risks

Trading monetary standards can be risky and complex. The interbank market has changing degrees of guideline, and Forex instruments are not institutionalized. In certain pieces of the world, Forex trading is totally unregulated.

The interbank market is comprised of banks trading with one another around the globe. The banks themselves need to decide and acknowledge sovereign risk and credit risk, and they have set up interior procedures to protect themselves as could be expected under the circumstances. Guidelines like this are industry forced for the insurance of each taking part bank.

Since the market is made by every one of the taking part banks giving offers and offers to a specific cash, the market valuing component depends on organic market. Since there are such huge exchange streams inside the framework, it is hard for rebel brokers to impact the cost of a money. This framework makes straightforwardness in the market for speculators with access to interbank managing.

Most little retail merchants exchange with generally little and semi-unregulated Forex intermediaries/vendors, which can (and once in a while do) re-quote costs and even exchange against their very own clients. Contingent upon where the vendor exists, there might be some administration and industry guideline, however those shields are conflicting the world over.

Most retail financial specialists ought to invest energy researching a Forex vendor to see if it is directed in the U.S. or on the other hand the U.K. (vendors in the U.S. what's more, U.K. have more oversight) or in a nation with careless guidelines and oversight. It is additionally a smart thought to discover what sort of account insurances are accessible if there should be an occurrence of a market emergency, or if a seller ends up bankrupt.

Masters and Challenges of Trading Forex

Master: The Forex markets are the biggest as far as every day trading volume the world and along these lines offer the most liquidity. This makes it simple to enter and leave a situation in any of the significant monetary forms inside a small amount of a second for a little spread in most economic situations.

Challenge: Banks, merchants and sellers in the Forex markets permit a high measure of influence, which implies that brokers can control enormous situations with generally minimal expenditure of their own. Influence in the scope of 100:1 is a high proportion yet normal in Forex. A dealer must comprehend the utilization of influence and the dangers that influence presents in an account. Extraordinary measures of influence have prompted numerous vendors getting to be wiped out of the blue.

Genius: The Forex market is exchanged 24 hours per day, five days per week—beginning every day in Australia and completion in New York. The significant focuses are Sydney, Hong Kong, Singapore, Tokyo, Frankfurt, Paris, London and New York.

Challenge: Trading monetary standards profitably requires a comprehension of financial essentials and markers. A cash broker needs to have a major picture comprehension of the economies of the different nations and their between connectedness to get a handle on the basics that drive money esteems.

Crucial STRATEGY

MAKING A TRADE: HOW TO BUY AND SELL CURRENCY

All Forex exchanges include two monetary standards since you're wagering on the estimation of a cash against another. Consider EUR/USD, the most-exchanged cash pair on the planet. EUR, the primary cash in the pair, is the base, and USD, the second, is the counter. At the point when you see a value cited on your foundation, that cost is the amount one euro is worth in US dollars. You generally observe two costs since one is the purchase cost and one is the sell. The contrast between the two is the spread. At the point when you snap purchase or sell, you are purchasing or selling the principal money in the pair.

FOREX TRANSACTION BA

Suppose you figure the euro will increment in incentive against the US dollar. Your pair is EUR/USD. Since the euro is first, and you figure it will go up, you purchase EUR/USD. In the event that you figure the euro will drop in an incentive against the US dollar, you sell EUR/USD. On the off chance that the EUR/USD purchase cost is 0.70644 and the sell cost is 0.70640, at that point the spread is 0.4 pips. On the off chance that the exchange moves your support (or against you), at that point, when you spread the spread, you could make a benefit (or misfortune) on your exchange.

Portions OF A PENNY: TRADING ON MARGIN

In the event that costs are cited to the hundredths of pennies, how might you see any huge profit for your speculation when you exchange Forex? The appropriate response is influence.

At the point when you exchange Forex, you're successfully acquiring the main money in the pair to purchase or sell the subsequent cash. With a US$5-trillion-a-day showcase, the liquidity is profound to the point that liquidity suppliers—the huge banks, essentially—enable you to exchange with influence. To exchange with influence, you just put in a safe spot the necessary edge for your exchange size. In case you're exchanging 200:1 influence, for instance, you can exchange $2,000 in the market while just putting aside $10 in edge in your trading account. For 50:1 influence, a similar exchange size would even now just require about £40 in edge. This gives you significantly more presentation, while holding your capital venture down.

Be that as it may, influence doesn't simply build your benefit potential. It can likewise build your misfortunes, which can surpass kept assets. At the point when you're new to Forex, you ought to consistently begin trading small amounts with lower influence proportions, until you feel good in the market.

- KNOW THE MARKET

Set aside the effort to consider cash sets and what influences them before taking a chance with your own capital; it's an interest in time that could spare you a decent measure of cash.

- MAKE A PLAN AND STICK TO IT

Making an trading plan is a basic segment of effective trading. It ought to incorporate your benefit objectives, risk resistance level, approach and assessment criteria. When you have an arrangement set up, ensure each exchange you think about falls inside your arrangement's parameters. Recollect that: you're likely most normal before you place an exchange and most nonsensical after your exchange is set

- PRACTICE

The best time to begin rehearsing is presently. The most ideal approach to figure out Forex trading is with no of the risk. Put your trading plan under serious scrutiny, to ensure genuine economic situations with risk free choices.

You'll get an opportunity to perceive what it resembles to exchange cash sets while taking your trading plan for a test drive without taking a chance with any of your own capital.

- FORECAST THE "Climate CONDITIONS" OF THE MARKET

Fruitful brokers should know about economic situations and plan appropriately. Major merchants like to exchange dependent on news and other money related and political information; specialized brokers incline toward specialized investigation devices, for example, Fibonacci retracements and different pointers to figure advertise developments. Most merchants utilize a mix of the two. Regardless of what your style, it is significant you utilize the instruments available to you to discover potential trading openings moving markets.

- KNOW YOUR LIMITS

This tip is a basic yet basic one that numerous dealers miss: know your breaking points. This incorporates realizing the amount you're willing to risk on each exchange, setting your influence proportion as per your needs, and failing to risk beyond what you can bear to lose.

- KNOW WHERE TO STOP ALONG THE WAY

You don't have the opportunity to sit and watch the business sectors each moment of consistently. You can all the more likely deal with your risk and ensure potential benefits through stop and point of confinement orders, getting you out of the market at the value you set.

Trailing stops are particularly useful; they trail your situation at a particular separation as the market moves, securing benefits should the market invert. Remember, notwithstanding, that putting in stop and cutoff requests may not really confine your risk for misfortunes.

- CHECK YOUR EMOTIONS AT THE DOOR

You have a vacant position and the market's not going your direction. Perhaps you could make it up with an exchange or two that don't fit with your trading plan... only a couple couldn't do any harm, correct? "Retribution trading" once in a while finishes well. Try not to give feeling a chance to hinder your arrangement for effective trading. At the point when you have a losing exchange, don't bet everything to attempt to make it in one shot; it's more astute to stay with your arrangement and make the lost back a little at once than to all of a sudden end up with two devastating misfortunes.

- KEEP IT SLOW AND STEADY

One key to trading is consistency. All dealers have lost cash, however on the off chance that you pursue your trading plan and take it an exchange at once, those misfortunes will probably present to a lesser degree a danger to your general technique. Teaching yourself and making an trading plan is great, yet the genuine test is adhering to that arrangement through tolerance and control.

- ### DON'T BE AFRAID TO EXPLORE

While consistency is significant, don't be reluctant to reexamine your trading plan if things aren't working like you thought they would. As your experience develops, your needs may change; your arrangement ought to consistently mirror your objectives. In the event that your objectives or money related circumstance changes, so should your arrangement.

- ### CHOOSE THE RIGHT TRADING PARTNER FOR YOU

It's basic to pick the correct trading partner as you draw in the Forex market. Estimating, execution, and the nature of client assistance would all be able to have any kind of effect as far as you can tell. So discover a pioneer in money exchanging and offers focused estimating, extraordinary client service and supportive aides and instructional exercises so you have a wide scope of apparatuses to begin exchanging on the Forex market.

Step by step instructions to BECOME A SMART INVESTOR

HEAD AND SHOULDERS

The head and shoulders graph example is famous and simple to spot example once a merchants know about what they are looking for. The example shows up on all occasions outlines and can in this manner be utilized by day and swing merchants just as speculators. Passage levels, stop levels and value targets make the development simple to actualize, as the diagram example gives significant and simple to-see levels. (Each time a financial specialist discusses getting in low or picking section and leave focuses, they are paying reverence to these men.

Step by step instructions to Trade The Head-And-Shoulders Pattern

What the Pattern Resembles

To start with, we'll take a gander at the arrangement of the head and shoulders design and the converse head and shoulders.

Head and Shoulders

Arrangement of the example:

- Left shoulder: Price rise pursued by a left value top, trailed by a decrease.
- Head: Price rise again shaping a higher pinnacle.
- Right shoulder: A decrease happens by and by, trailed by an ascent framing the correct pinnacle which is lower than the head.

Developments are once in a while immaculate, which means there might be some clamor between the separate shoulders and head.

Figure 1: SOLF Daily Chart – Head and Shoulders

Converse Head and Shoulders

- Formation of the example:
- Left shoulder: Price decreases and moves higher.
- Head: Another decrease jumps out at a lower level.
- Right shoulder: Price at that point moves higher and moves back lower, however not as low as the head.

Once more, arrangements are once in a while immaculate. There might be some market commotion between the particular shoulders and head.

Figure 2: SPY Daily Chart – Inverse Head and Shoulders

Source: Think or Swim – TD Ameritrade

Putting the Neckline

The initial step is to find the left shoulder, head and right shoulder on the outline. In the standard head and shoulders design (showcase top), we interface the low after the left shoulder with the low made after the head. This makes our "neck area" – the yellow line on the graphs. We'll talk about the significance of the neck area in the accompanying segment. In a reverse head and shoulders design, we interface the high after the left shoulder with the high framed after the head, along these lines making our neck area for this example.

The most widely recognized passage is the point at which a breakout happens – the neck area is broken and an exchange is taken. Another section point requires more tolerance and accompanies the likelihood that the move might be missed all together. This strategy includes sitting tight for a pullback to the neck area after a breakout has just happened. This is progressively preservationist in that we can check whether the pullback stops and the first breakout course continues, however it likewise implies the exchange might be missed if the value continues moving in the breakout heading. The two strategies are appeared in Figure 3.

Figure 3: SPY Daily Chart – Possible passage focuses

Setting Your Stops

In the customary market top example, the stops are set simply over the correct shoulder (besting design) after the neck area is infiltrated. Then again, the leader of the example can be utilized as a stop, yet this is likely a lot greater risk and consequently diminishes the reward to risk to proportion of the example. In the converse example, the stop is put just beneath the correct shoulder. Once more, the stop can be put at the leader of the example, in spite of the fact that this exposes the broker to more serious risk. In Figure 3, the stop would be set at $104 (just beneath right shoulder) when the exchange was taken.

Setting Your Profit Targets

The benefit focus at the example is the cost distinction between the head and depressed spot of either shoulder. This distinction is then subtracted from the neck area breakout level (at a market top) to give a value focus to the drawback. For a market base, the thing that matters is added to the neck area breakout cost to give a value focus to the upside.

As SPY is a vigorously exchanged ETF speaking to the more extensive market, the benefit focus for the opposite head and shoulders design in Figure 2 would be:

$113.20 (this is the high after left shoulder) – $101.13 (this is the low of the head) = $12.07

This distinction is then added to the breakout cost (subtracted on account of a standard head and shoulders design). The breakout cost is directly around $113.25, giving us a benefit focus of $125.32 ($113.25 + $12.07).

Now and then, financial specialists need to hold up quite a while – as long as a while – between detecting the breakout and arriving at the perfect benefit target. (Checking your exchanges constant can enable you to foresee their results.

Why the Head and Shoulders Pattern Works

No example is flawless, nor does it work inevitably. However there are a few reasons why the diagram design hypothetically works (the market top will be utilized for this thinking, yet it applies to both):

- As value tumbles from the market high (head), merchants have started to enter the market and there is less forceful purchasing.

- As the neck area is drawn nearer, numerous individuals who purchased in the last wave higher or purchased on the assembly in the correct shoulder are currently refuted and confronting enormous misfortunes – it is this huge gathering that will presently leave positions, driving the cost toward the benefit target.

- The stop over the correct shoulder is sensible in light of the fact that the pattern has moved downwards – the correct shoulder is a lower high than the head – and subsequently the correct shoulder is probably not going to be broken until an upswing resumes.

- The benefit target expect that the individuals who aren't right or acquired the security at a poor time will be compelled to leave their positions, in this way making an inversion of comparable size to the fixing design that just happened.

- The neck area is the time when numerous brokers are encountering torment and will be compelled to leave positions, in this way pushing the cost toward the value target.

- Volume can be looked too. During reverse head and shoulder designs (advertise bottoms), we would in a perfect world like the volume to extend as a breakout happens. This shows expanded purchasing interest that will push cost toward the objective. Diminishing volume shows absence of enthusiasm for the upside move and warrants some distrust.

The Pitfalls of Trading Head and Shoulders

As expressed, the example isn't immaculate. Here are some potential issues with exchanging a head and shoulders design:

- You need to discover examples and watch them grow, however you ought not exchange this methodology until the example is finished. So it could mean an extensive stretch of pausing.

- It won't work constantly. The stop levels will be hit at times.
- The benefit target won't generally be come to, so merchants may wish to tweak how market factors will influence their exit from the security.
- The example isn't constantly tradable. For instance, if there is a huge drop on one of the shoulders because of an eccentric occasion, at that point the determined value targets will probably not be hit.
- Patterns can be abstract. One merchant may see a shoulder, where another doesn't. When trading designs, characterize what establishes an example for you previously – given the general rules above.

The Bottom Line

Head and shoulder examples happen on all occasions outlines, and can be seen outwardly. While abstract now and again, the total example gives passages, stops and benefit targets, making it simple to execute a trading methodology. The example is made out of a left shoulder, head, at that point pursued by a correct shoulder. The most widely recognized section point is a breakout of the neck area, with a stop above (showcase top) or underneath (advertise base) the correct shoulder. The benefit target is the distinction of the high and low with the example included (advertise base) or subtracted (showcase top) from the breakout cost. The framework isn't flawless, yet it provides a technique for trading the business sectors dependent on consistent value developments. (Benefit accepting open doors flourish utilizing this lesser-known example

CUP HANDLE

What Is A Cup And Handle?

A cup and handle value design on bar outlines is a specialized marker that takes after a cup and handle where the cup is in the state of a "U" and the handle has a slight descending float. The right-hand side of the example regularly has low trading volume, and might be as short as seven weeks or up to 65 weeks.

What's a Cup and Handle?

KEY TAKEAWAYS

* A cup and handle value design on bar outlines takes after a cup and handle where the cup is in the state of a "U" and the handle has a slight descending float.
* A cup and handle is viewed as a bullish continuation design and is utilized to distinguish purchasing openings.
* Traders should put in a stop purchase request somewhat over the upper pattern line of the handle.

What Does A Cup And Handle Tell You?

American expert William J. O'Neil characterized the cup and handle (C&H) design in his 1988 great, "How to Make Money in Stocks," including specialized necessities through a progression of articles distributed in Investor's Business Daily, which he established in 1984. O'Neil included time period estimations for every segment, just as a nitty gritty portrayal of the adjusted lows that give the example it's one of a kind tea cup appearance.

As a stock framing this example tests old highs, it is probably going to cause selling weight from financial specialists who recently purchased at those levels; selling weight is probably going to cause cost to solidify with an inclination toward a downtrend pattern for a time of four days to about a month, prior progressing higher. A cup and handle is viewed as a bullish continuation design and is utilized to distinguish purchasing openings.

It merits considering the accompanying when distinguishing cup and handle designs:

Length - Generally, cups with longer and that's only the tip of the iceberg "U" molded bottoms give a more grounded sign. Keep away from cups with a sharp "V" bottoms.

Profundity - Ideally, the cup ought not be excessively profound. Dodge handles that are excessively profound additionally, as handles should shape in the top portion of the cup design.

Volume - Volume should diminish as costs decrease and remain lower than normal in the base of the bowl; it should then increment when the stock starts to make its move higher, back up to test the past high.

A retest of past obstruction isn't required to contact or go in close vicinity to a few ticks of the old high; in any case, the further the highest point of the handle is away from the highs, the more huge the breakout should be.

Case Of How To Use The Cup And Handle

The picture beneath portrays a great cup and handle development. Put in a stop purchase request marginally over the upper pattern line of the handle. Request execution should possibly happen if the value breaks the example's obstruction. Brokers may encounter overabundance slippage and enter a bogus breakout utilizing a forceful section. Then again, trust that the cost will close over the upper pattern line of the handle, in this manner put in a point of confinement request somewhat beneath the example's breakout level, endeavoring to get an execution if the value backtracks. There is a danger of missing the exchange if the value keeps on progressing and doesn't draw back.

A benefit target is dictated by estimating the separation between the base of the cup and the example's breakout level, and expanding that separation upward from the breakout. For instance, if the separation between the base of the cup and handle breakout level is 20 points, a benefit target is put 20 points over the example's handle. Stop misfortune requests might be set either underneath the handle or beneath the cup contingent upon the broker's risk resilience and market unpredictability.

Presently we should consider a genuine authentic model utilizing Wynn Resorts, Limited (WYNN), which opened up to the world on the Nasdaq trade close $13 in October 2002 and rose to $154 five years after the fact. The ensuing decrease finished inside two of the first sale of stock (IPO) cost, far surpassing O'Neil's necessity for a shallow cup high in the earlier pattern. The resulting recuperation wave arrived at the earlier high in 2011, about 10 years after the principal print. The handle pursues the great pullback desire, discovering support at the half retracement in an adjusted shape, and comes back to the high for a second time 14 months after the fact. The stock broke out in October 2013 and included 90 in the accompanying five months.

Restrictions Of The Cup And Handle

Like every single specialized pointer, the cup and handle ought to be utilized working together with different sign and markers before settling on an trading choice. Explicitly with the cup and handle, certain impediments have been distinguished by experts. First is that it can require some investment for the example to completely shape, which can prompt late choices. While multi month to 1 year is the normal time period for a cup and handle to frame, it can likewise happen rapidly or take quite a long while to build up itself, making it questionable at times. Another issue has to do with the profundity of the cup some portion of the development. At times a shallower cup can be a sign, while different occasions a profound cup can deliver a bogus sign. Once in a while the cup structures without the trademark handle. At long last, one restriction shared crosswise over numerous specialized examples is that it tends to be inconsistent in illiquid stocks.

WEDGES

On the specialized examination outline, a wedge example is a market pattern regularly found in exchanged resources (stocks, securities, prospects, and so on.). The example is portrayed by a contracting range in costs combined with an upward pattern in costs (known as a rising wedge) or a descending pattern in costs (known as a falling wedge).

A wedge example is viewed as an example which is framing at the top or base of the pattern. It is a sort of development where trading exercises are bound to combining straight lines which structure an example. It should take around 3 to about a month to finish the wedge. This example has a rising or falling inclination pointing a similar way. It varies from the triangle as in both limit lines either slant up or down. Value breaking out point makes another distinction from the triangle. Falling and rising wedges are a little piece of halfway or significant pattern. As they are saved for minor patterns, they are not viewed as significant examples. When that fundamental or essential pattern resumes itself, the wedge example loses its viability as a specialized pointer.

FALLING EDGE

The falling wedge example is described by a diagram design which structures when the market makes lower lows and lower highs with a contracting range. At the point when this example is found in a descending pattern, it is viewed as an inversion design, as the withdrawal of the range shows the downtrend is losing steam. At the point when this example is found in an upswing, it is viewed as a bullish example, as the market range progresses toward becoming smaller into the rectification, demonstrating that the descending pattern is losing quality and the resumption of the upturn is really taking shape.

In a falling wedge, both limit lines inclination down from left to right. The upper drops at a more extreme point than the lower line. Volume continues decreasing and trading action backs off because of narrowing costs. There comes the limit, and trade movement after the breakout varies. When costs move out of the particular limit lines of a falling wedge, they are bound to move sideways and saucer-out before they continue the essential pattern.

RISING EDGE

The rising wedge example is described by a diagram design which structures when the market makes higher highs and higher lows with a contracting range. At the point when this example is found in an upswing, it is viewed as an inversion design, as the constriction of the range shows that the upturn is losing quality. At the point when this example is found in a downtrend, it is viewed as a bearish example, as the market range moves toward becoming smaller into the remedy, showing that the amendment is losing quality, and that the resumption of the downtrend is really taking shape.

In a rising wedge, both limit lines inclination up from left to right. Albeit the two lines point a similar way, the lower line ascends at a more extreme edge than the upper one. Costs for the most part decay in the wake of getting through the lower limit line. To the extent volumes are concerned, they continue declining with each new value advance or wave up, demonstrating that the interest is debilitating at the more significant expense level. A rising wedge is increasingly dependable when found in a bearish market. In a bullish pattern what is by all accounts a Rising Wedge may really be a Flag or a Pennant (stepbrother of a wedge) requiring around about a month to finish.

Twofold AND TRIPLE TOP

A twofold top is an incredibly bearish specialized inversion design that structures after a benefit arrives at a significant expense two back to back occasions with a moderate decay between the two highs. It is affirmed once the advantage's value falls beneath a help level equivalent to the low between the two earlier highs.

The triple top example is a sort of diagram example utilized in specialized examination to anticipate the inversion of an upturn. The example happens when the cost of an advantage makes three tops at about a similar value level. The territory of the pinnacles is obstruction. The pullbacks between the pinnacles are known as the swing lows. After the third pinnacle, if the value falls beneath the swing lows, the example is viewed as complete and brokers watch for a further move to the drawback.

Twofold (or triple) tops (or bottoms)

These outline examples propose a powerless pattern or an inversion of forex costs. in the forex or upsetting. Step by step, as the example is framed, exchange volumes continuously decline. A twofold or triple top arrangement gives a decent sign to close a long position and the other way around for the twofold or triple base, which gives a sign to close a short position. Pullbacks and return are basic after a leap forward the affirmation line. Forex dealers can likewise start a short position when the affirmation line has been gotten through to wager on a pattern inversion, with a stop set over the past top.

Twofold and triple tops create in an upswing, they comprise of a few value tops at the equivalent inexact level.

The twofold or triple bottoms, then again, create in downtrends.

There are two kinds of tops and bottoms: the adjusted "Eve" shapes, and "Adam" shapes, which comprise of a solitary candle or pinnacle.

TRAPS

A bull trap is a bogus sign, alluding to a declining pattern in a stock, file or other security that turns around after a persuading rally and breaks an earlier help level. The move "traps" merchants or financial specialists that followed up on the purchase signal and produces misfortunes on coming about long positions. A bull trap may likewise allude to a whipsaw design.

- A bull trap signifies an inversion that powers showcase members on an inappropriate side of value activity to leave positions with sudden misfortunes.
- Bull traps happen when purchasers neglect to help an assembly over a breakout level.
- Traders and financial specialists can bring down the recurrence of bull traps by looking for affirmation finishing a breakout specialized pointers or potentially design divergences.
- The inverse of a bull trap is a bear trap, which happens when dealers neglect to press a decay beneath a breakdown level.

What Does a Bull Trap Tell You?

A bull trap happens when a merchant or speculator purchases a security that breaks out over an obstruction level - a typical specialized examination based system. While numerous breakouts are trailed by solid moves higher, the security may rapidly invert heading. These are known as "bull traps" since brokers and financial specialists who purchased the breakout are "caught" in the exchange.

Dealers and speculators can keep away from bull traps by searching for affirmations following a breakout. For instance, a dealer may search for higher than normal volume and bullish candles following a breakout to affirm that cost is probably going to move higher. A breakout that creates low volume and hesitant candles -, for example, a doji star - could be an indication of a bull trap.

From a mental angle, bull traps happen when bulls neglect to help a meeting over a breakout level, which could be because of an absence of energy as well as benefit taking. Bears may hop on the chance to sell the security in the event that they see divergences, dropping costs beneath obstruction levels, which would then be able to trigger stop-misfortune orders.

The most ideal approach to deal with bull traps is to perceive notice signs early, for example, low volume breakouts, and leave the exchange as fast as could be expected under the circumstances if a bull trap is suspected. Stop-misfortune requests can be useful in these conditions, particularly if the market is moving rapidly, to abstain from giving feeling a chance to drive basic leadership.

Case of How Bull Trap Works

In this model, the security auctions and hits another 52-week low before bouncing back forcefully on high volume and lifting into trendline opposition. Numerous dealers and speculators hop on to the move, envisioning a breakout above trendline opposition yet the security inverts at obstruction and diverts pointedly lower from these levels. New bulls get caught in long exchanges and cause quick misfortunes, except if forceful risk the executives strategies are embraced.

The dealer or speculator could have stayed away from the bull trap by trusting that a breakout will unfurl before buying the security, or if nothing else moderated misfortunes by setting a tight stop-misfortune request just beneath the breakout level.

Trading AND NEWS

Consider the possibility that there was an approach to make cash immediately regardless of whether you had no clue whether the market would go up or down.

It's conceivable insofar as there is adequate value instability.

Also, when would you be able to get this instability? At the point when news like financial information or national bank declarations is discharged!

The principal interesting point is which news reports to exchange.

In a perfect world, you would need to just exchange those reports on the grounds that there is a high likelihood the market will make a major move after their discharge.

The following thing you ought to do is investigate the range in any event 20 minutes before the genuine news discharge.

The high of that range will be your upper breakout point, and the low of that range will be your lower breakout point.

Note that the littler the range is the more probable it is you will see a major move from the news report.

The breakout focuses will be your entrance levels.

This is the place you need to set your requests. Your stops ought to be set around 20 pips underneath or more the breakout focuses, and your underlying targets ought to be about equivalent to the scope of the breakout levels.

Straddle Trade

This is known as a straddle exchange.

You are hoping to play BOTH sides of the exchanges.

It doesn't make a difference which bearing the value moves, the straddle procedure will have you situated to exploit it.

Since you're set up to enter the market in either heading, you should simply trust that the news will turn out.

Here and there you may get activated one way just to find that you get halted out on the grounds that the value rapidly turns around the other way.

Be that as it may, your other passage will get activated and if that exchange wins, you ought to recover your underlying misfortunes and turn out with a little benefit.

A most ideal situation would be that just one of your exchanges gets activated and the value keeps on moving in support of you with the goal that you don't bring about any misfortunes.

In any case, whenever done effectively you should in any case end up positive for the afternoon.

Guideline INDICATORS

Pointers, for example, moving midpoints and Bollinger Bands®, are numerically based specialized investigation instruments that merchants and speculators use to break down the past and anticipate future value patterns and examples. Where fundamentalists may follow financial reports and yearly reports, specialized brokers depend on pointers to help translate the market. The objective in utilizing pointers is to recognize trade openings. For instance, a moving normal hybrid frequently predicts a pattern change. In this case, applying the moving normal marker to a value diagram enables brokers to recognize regions where the pattern may change.

Financial Indicators

Procedures, then again, every now and again utilize pointers in a target way to decide passage, exit and additionally exchange the board rules. A procedure is a complete arrangement of guidelines that indicates the definite conditions under which exchanges will be set up, oversaw and shut. Procedures regularly incorporate the point by point utilization of markers or, all the more much of the time, various markers, to build up occasions where exchanging action will happen. (Delve further into moving midpoints. Peruse: Simple versus Exponential Moving Averages.)

While this book doesn't concentrate on a particular trading procedures, it fills in as a clarification of how pointers and systems are unique, and how they cooperate to enable specialized experts to pinpoint high-likelihood trading arrangements. (For additional information, look at: Create Your Own Trading Strategies.)

Pointers

A developing number of specialized pointers are accessible for brokers to consider, incorporating those in the open area, for example, a moving normal or the stochastic oscillator, just as financially accessible exclusive markers. Also, numerous brokers build up their own extraordinary pointers, some of the time with the help of a certified software engineer. Most markers have client characterized factors that enable merchants to adjust key sources of info, for example, the "think back period" (how much chronicled information will be utilized to frame the figurings) to suit their needs.

A moving normal, for instance, is just a normal of a security's cost over a specific period. The timespan is determined in the sort of moving normal; for example, a 50-day moving normal. This moving normal will average the earlier 50 days of value action, for the most part utilizing the security's end cost in its figuring (however other value focuses, for example, the open, high or low, can be utilized). The client characterizes the length of the moving normal just as the value point that will be utilized in the figuring. (To find out additional, see our Moving Averages Tutorial.)

Techniques

A technique is a lot of target, outright principles characterizing when a broker will make a move. Ordinarily, procedures incorporate both exchange channels and triggers, the two of which are frequently founded on markers. Exchange channels recognize the arrangement conditions; exchange triggers distinguish precisely when a specific move ought to be made. An exchange channel, for instance, may be a value that has shut over its 200-day moving normal. This makes way for the exchange trigger, which is the real condition that prompts the broker to act – AKA, the line in the sand. An exchange trigger may be when value arrives at one tick over the bar that broke the 200-day moving normal.

All things considered, a methodology isn't just "Purchase when value moves over the moving normal." This is excessively shifty and doesn't give any complete subtleties to making a move. Here are instances of certain inquiries that should be offered an explanation to make a goal procedure:

- What sort of moving normal will be utilized, including length and value point to be utilized in the computation?
- How far over the moving normal does value need to move?
- Should the exchange be entered when value moves a predetermined separation over the moving normal, at the end of the bar or at the open of the following bar?
- What kind of request will be utilized to put the exchange? Point of confinement? Market?
- How numerous agreements or offers will be exchanged?
- What are the cash the board rules?
- What are the leave rules?

These inquiries must be offered an explanation to build up a succinct arrangement of guidelines to shape a technique.

What Is Relative Strength Index – RSI?

The Relative Strength Index (RSI) is an energy marker that estimates the size of late value changes to assess overbought or oversold conditions in the cost of a stock or other resource. The RSI is shown as an oscillator (a line chart that moves between two boundaries) and can have a perusing from 0 to 100. The marker was initially created by J. Welles Wilder Jr. furthermore, presented in his fundamental 1978 book, New Concepts in Technical Trading Systems.

Conventional understanding and utilization of the RSI are that estimations of 70 or above show that a security is getting to be overbought or exaggerated and might be prepared for a pattern inversion or restorative pullback in cost. An RSI perusing of 30 or underneath shows an oversold or underestimated condition.

The Formula for RSI

The relative quality list (RSI) is figured with a two-section count that starts with the accompanying equation:

The normal increase or misfortune utilized in the count is the normal rate addition or misfortunes during a think back period. The recipe utilizes positive qualities for the normal misfortunes.

The standard is to utilize 14 periods to figure the underlying RSI esteem. For instance, envision the market finished higher seven off of the previous 14 days with a normal addition of 1%. The staying seven days all shut lower with a normal loss of - 0.8%. The count for the initial segment of the RSI would resemble the accompanying extended estimation:

Once there are 14 times of information accessible, the second piece of the RSI recipe can be determined. The second step of the figuring smooths the outcomes.

The RSI will ascend as the number and size of positive closes increment, and it will fall as the number and size of misfortunes increment. The second piece of the figuring smooths the outcome, so the RSI will just close to 100 or 0 out of a firmly drifting business sector.

As should be obvious in the above diagram, the RSI pointer can stay in "overbought" region for broadened periods while stock is in an upswing. The pointer can remain in "oversold" domain for quite a while stock is in a downtrend. This can be mistaking for new experts, yet figuring out how to utilize the marker inside the setting of the overarching pattern will explain these issues

RSI Swing Rejections Example

Another trading procedure looks at the RSI's conduct when it is reappearing from overbought or oversold region. This sign is known as a bullish "swing dismissal" and has four sections:

1. RSI falls into oversold region.
2. RSI crosses back above 30%.
3. RSI structures another plunge without intersection once again into oversold domain.
4. RSI at that point breaks its latest high.

As should be obvious in the accompanying graph, the RSI pointer was oversold, down and out up through 30% and shaped the dismissal low that set off the sign when it bobbed higher. Utilizing the RSI along these lines is fundamentally the same as drawing trendlines on a value graph.

Like divergences, there is a bearish form of the swing dismissal signal that resembles a perfect representation of the bullish variant. A bearish swing dismissal likewise has four sections:

1. RSI ascents into overbought region.
2. RSI crosses back underneath 70%.
3. RSI structures another high without intersection once again into overbought domain.
4. RSI at that point breaks its latest low.

MOVING AVERAGE

A moving normal (MA) is a generally utilized pointer in specialized investigation that enables smooth out cost to activity by sifting through the "clamor" from irregular transient value vacillations. It is a pattern following, or slacking, marker since it depends on past costs.

The two essential and normally utilized moving midpoints are the basic moving normal (SMA), which is the straightforward normal of a security over a characterized number of timeframes, and the exponential moving normal (EMA), which gives more prominent load to later costs.

The most widely recognized uses of moving midpoints are to distinguish the pattern bearing and to decide backing and opposition levels. While moving midpoints are helpful enough all alone, they likewise structure the reason for other specialized pointers, for example, the moving normal intermingling disparity (MACD).

Since we have broad definitions and articles around explicit sorts of moving midpoints, we will just characterize the expression "moving normal" for the most part here.

The Formulas For Moving Averages Are

Basic Moving Average

The basic moving normal computes the number-crunching mean of a security over a number (n) of timeframes, A.

Exponential Moving Average

To ascertain an EMA, you should initially process the basic moving normal (SMA) over a specific timeframe. Next, you should ascertain the multiplier for weighting the EMA (the smoothing), which normally pursues the recipe: [2 ÷ (chose timeframe + 1)]. Along these lines, for a 20-day moving normal, the multiplier would be [2/(20+1)]= 0.0952. At that point you utilize the smoothing variable joined with the past EMA to land at the present worth. The EMA therefore gives a higher weighting to ongoing costs, while the SMA appoints equivalent weighting to all qualities.

What Do Moving Averages Tell You?

Moving midpoints linger behind current value activity since they depend on past costs; the more drawn out the timeframe for the moving normal, the more prominent the slack. In this manner, a 200-day MA will have a lot more noteworthy level of slack than a 20-day MA since it contains costs for as long as 200 days.

The length of the moving normal to utilize relies upon the trade targets, with shorter moving midpoints utilized for transient trading and longer-term moving midpoints progressively appropriate for long haul financial specialists. The 50-day and 200-day MAs are broadly trailed by financial specialists and brokers, with breaks above and underneath this moving normal viewed as significant trade signals.

Moving midpoints additionally confer significant trade signals without anyone else, or when two midpoints traverse. A rising moving normal demonstrates that the security is in an upswing, while a declining moving normal shows that it is in a downtrend.

Likewise, upward force is affirmed with a bullish hybrid, which happens when a momentary moving normal crosses over a more drawn out term moving normally. Descending energy is affirmed with a bearish hybrid, which happens when a momentary moving normal crosses underneath a more extended term moving normally.

Foreseeing patterns in the securities exchange is no basic procedure. While you cannot anticipate what will happen precisely, you can give yourself better chances utilizing specialized examination and research. Putting your exploration and specialized examination to the test in the market would require an investment fund. Picking a specialist can be disappointing because of the assortment among them, however you can pick a standout amongst other online stockbrokers to locate the correct stage for your needs.

Moving midpoints are an absolutely adaptable marker, which implies that the client can openly pick whatever time allotment they need when making the normal. The most widely recognized timespans utilized in moving midpoints are 15, 20, 30, 50, 100, and 200 days. The shorter the time length used to make the normal, the more delicate it will be to value changes. The more drawn out the time length, the less delicate, or progressively smoothed out, the normal will be.

There is no "right" time allotment to utilize when setting up your moving midpoints. The most ideal approach to make sense of which one works best for you is to explore different avenues regarding various distinctive timeframes until you discover one that accommodates your methodology.

STOCHASTIC

Stochastic alludes to an arbitrarily decided process.[1] The word initially showed up in English to depict a numerical item called a stochastic procedure, yet now in arithmetic the terms stochastic procedure and irregular procedure are viewed as exchangeable.

The term stochastic is utilized in various fields, especially where stochastic or arbitrary procedures are utilized to speak to frameworks or wonders that appear to change in an irregular manner.

It is likewise utilized in account, because of apparently irregular changes in money related markets just as in medication, semantics, music, media, shading hypothesis, herbal science, assembling, and geomorphology.

In the late 1950s, George Lane created stochastics, a marker that estimates the connection between an issue's end cost and its value extend over a foreordained timeframe.

Fourteen is the numerical number utilized in the time mode. Contingent upon the professional's objective, it can speak to days, weeks, or months. The chartist might need to analyze a whole part. For a long haul perspective on a segment, the chartist would begin by taking a gander at 14 months of the whole business' trade range.

Value Action

Stochastics is a favored specialized pointer since it is straightforward and has a high level of precision. It is utilized to indicate when a stock has moved into an overbought or oversold position.

The reason of stochastics is that when a stock patterns upwards, its end price tends to exchange at the high day's end range or value activity. Value activity alludes to the scope of costs at which a stock exchanges all through the day by day session. For instance, if a stock opened at $10, exchanged as low as $9.75 and as high as $10.75, at that point shut at $10.50 for the afternoon, the value activity or range would be between $9.75 (the low of the day) and $10.75 (the high of the day). Alternately, if the cost has a descending development, the end value will in general exchange at or close to the low scope of the day's trading session.

Relative Strength Index

Jack D. Schwager, the prime supporter of Fund Seeder and writer of a few books on specialized examination, utilizes the expression "standardized" to portray stochastic oscillators that have foreordained limits, both on the high and low sides. A case of such an oscillator is the relative quality list (RSI)— a mainstream force pointer utilized in specialized investigation—which has a scope of 0 to 100. It is typically set at either the 20 to 80 territory or the 30 to 70 territory. Regardless of whether you're taking a gander at an area or an individual issue, it tends to be useful to utilize stochastics and the RSI related to one another.

Stochastics: An Accurate Buy And Sell Indicator

Equation

Stochastics is estimated with the K line and the D line. In any case, it is the D line that we pursue intently, for it will show any significant flag in the outline. Numerically, the K line resembles this:

The equation for the more significant D line resembles this:

We demonstrate to you these recipes for the wellbeing of interest as it were. The present outlining programming does every one of the counts, making the entire specialized examination process so a lot simpler, and accordingly, additionally energizing for the normal speculator.

Perusing the Chart

The K line is quicker than the D line—the more slow of the two. The financial specialist needs to look as the D line and the cost of the issue start to change and move into either the overbought (over the 80 line) or the oversold (under the 20 line) positions. The financial specialist needs to consider selling the stock when the marker moves over the 80 level. On the other hand, the speculator needs to consider purchasing an issue that is underneath the 20 line and is beginning to climb with expanded volume.

Throughout the years, numerous articles have investigated "tweaking" this pointer. Be that as it may, new financial specialists should focus on the nuts and bolts of stochastics.

In the diagram of eBay over, various clear purchasing chances introduced themselves over the spring and summer a long time of 2001. There are additionally various sell pointers that would have drawn the consideration of momentary brokers. The solid purchase signal toward the beginning of April would have given the two speculators and brokers an extraordinary 12-day run, going from the mid $30 territory to the mid $50 region.

The Bottom Line

Stochastics is a most loved pointer of certain professionals due to the precision of its discoveries. It is effectively seen both via prepared veterans and new experts, and it will in general help all financial specialists settle on great passage and leave choices on their property. (For more understanding, read "Investigating Oscillators and Indicators: Stochastic Oscillator.")

BOLLIGER BANDS

Bollinger Bands, a diagram marker created by John Bollinger, are utilized to quantify a market's instability.

Fundamentally, this little apparatus reveals to us whether the market is tranquil or whether the market is LOUD!

At the point when the market is calm, the groups contract and when the market is LOUD, the groups extend.

Notice on the diagram underneath that when cost is tranquil, the groups are near one another. At the point when value climbs, the groups spread separated.

It's just as simple as that. Truly, we could go on and bore you by going into the historical backdrop of the Bollinger Band, how it is determined, the scientific recipes behind it, et cetera, however we truly didn't want to type it full scale.

Believe it or not, you don't have to know any of that garbage. We believe it's progressively significant that we demonstrate to you a few different ways you can apply the Bollinger Bands to your trading.

Note: If you truly need to find out about the counts of a Bollinger Band, look at John's book, Bollinger on Bollinger Bands.

The Bollinger Bounce

One thing you should think about Bollinger Bands is that value will in general come back to the center of the groups. That is the entire thought behind the "Bollinger Bounce."

By taking a gander at the diagram underneath, would you be able to disclose to us where the cost may go straightaway?

On the off chance that you said down, at that point you are right! As should be obvious, the value settled down towards the center region of the groups.

What you just observed was an exemplary Bollinger Bounce. The explanation these bobs happen is on the grounds that Bollinger groups act like powerful help and opposition levels.

The more extended the time allotment you are in, the more grounded these groups will in general be.

Numerous dealers have created frameworks that flourish with these skips and this technique is best utilized when the market is running and there is no unmistakable pattern.

Presently how about we take a gander at an approach to utilize Bollinger Bands when the market is TRENDING...

Bollinger Squeeze and Break Out

The "Bollinger Squeeze" is really plain as day. At the point when the groups crush together, it ordinarily implies that a breakout is preparing to occur.

On the off chance that the candles begin to break out over the TOP band, at that point the move will for the most part keep on going UP.

In the event that the candles begin to break out beneath the BOTTOM band, at that point cost will as a rule keep on going DOWN.

Taking a gander at the outline above, you can see the groups crushing together. The cost has quite recently begun to break out of the top band. In light of this data, where do you figure the cost will go?

In the event that you said up, you are right once more!

This is the manner by which an ordinary Bollinger Squeeze works.

This technique is intended for you to get a move as right on time as could be expected under the circumstances.

Arrangements like these don't happen each day, however you can presumably spot them a couple of times each week on the off chance that you are taking a gander at a 15-minute diagram.

There are numerous different things you can do with Bollinger Bands, however these are the two most regular methodologies related with them.

It's a great opportunity to place this in your dealer's tool kit before we proceed onward to the following pointer.

MACD is an abbreviation for Moving Average Convergence Divergence.

This apparatus is utilized to recognize moving midpoints that are demonstrating another pattern, regardless of whether it's bullish or bearish.

All things considered, our top need in trading is having the option to discover a pattern, since that is the place where most cash is made.

With a MACD graph, you will more often than not observe three numbers that are utilized for its settings.

- The first is the quantity of periods that is utilized to ascertain the quicker moving normal.
- The second is the quantity of periods that is utilized in the more slow moving normal.
- And the third is the quantity of bars that is utilized to figure the moving normal of the contrast between the quicker and more slow moving midpoints.
- For instance, if you somehow happened to see "12, 26, 9" as the MACD parameters (which is normally the default setting for most diagramming programming), this is the manner by which you would translate it:

- The 12 speaks to the past 12 bars of the quicker moving normal.
- The 26 speaks to the past 26 bars of the more slow moving normal.
- The 9 speaks to the past 9 bars of the distinction between the two moving midpoints. This is plotted by vertical lines called a histogram (the green lines in the graph above).

There is a typical misguided judgment with regards to the lines of the MACD.

The two lines that are drawn are NOT moving midpoints of the cost. Rather, they are the moving midpoints of the DIFFERENCE between two moving midpoints.

In our model over, the quicker moving normal is the moving normal of the distinction between the 12 and 26-period moving midpoints.

The more slow moving normal plots the normal of the past MACD line. By and by, from our model over, this would be a 9-period moving normal.

This implies we are taking the normal of the last 9 times of the quicker MACD line and plotting it as our more slow moving normal.

This smoothens out the first line significantly more, which gives us an increasingly precise line.

The histogram just plots the distinction between the quick and moderate moving normal.

On the off chance that you take a gander at our unique diagram, you can see that, as the two moving midpoints isolated, the histogram gets greater.

This is called dissimilarity on the grounds that the quicker moving normal is "veering" or moving endlessly from the more slow moving normal.

As the drawing midpoints get nearer to one another, the histogram gets littler. This is called union on the grounds that the quicker moving normal is "merging" or drawing nearer to the more slow moving normal.

Also, that, old buddy, is the means by which you get the name, Moving Average Convergence Divergence! Whew, we have to break our knuckles after that one!

Alright, so now you comprehend what MACD does. Presently we'll demonstrate to you what MACD can accomplish for YOU.

The most effective method to Trade Using MACD

Since there are two moving midpoints with various "speeds", the quicker one will clearly be faster to respond to value development than the more slow one.

At the point when another pattern happens, the quick line will respond first and inevitably cross the more slow line. At the point when this "hybrid" happens, and the quick line begins to "veer" or move away from the more slow line, it regularly demonstrates that another pattern has framed.

From the diagram above, you can see that the quick line crossed under the moderate line and accurately recognized another downtrend.

Notice that when the lines crossed, the histogram briefly vanishes.

This is on the grounds that the contrast between the lines at the hour of the cross is 0.

As the downtrend starts and the quick line separates from the moderate line, the histogram gets greater, which is great sign of a solid pattern.

We should investigate a model.

In EUR/USD's 1-hour graph over, the quick line crossed over the moderate line while the histogram vanished. This proposed the brief downtrend would in the long run invert.

From that point, EUR/USD started shooting up as it began another upswing. Suppose you went long after the hybrid, you would've picked up just about 200 pips!

There is one downside to MACD. Normally, moving midpoints will in general linger behind cost. All things considered, it's only a normal of verifiable costs.

Since the MACD speaks to moving midpoints of other moving midpoints and is smoothed out by another moving normal, you can envision that there is a lot of slack. Nonetheless, MACD is as yet one of the most supported devices by numerous dealers.

CHAPTER THREE
WHAT IS THE BEST INDICATOR?

◆ ◆ ◆

The issue is that, from the start locate, names of specialized markers can sound obnoxiously entangled, for instance, MACD, RSI or Stochastic. In any case, we prescribe you not to pass judgment flippantly. We will give you a reasonable and straightforward clarification of the most well-known specialized markers. We ensure that you will see how to utilize them. Is it true that you are intrigued? How about we start at that point!

Do specialized markers really work?

We exchange to get a positive outcome or, as it were, benefit. Numerous learner dealers are anxious to know whether specialized markers can give them great trade signals.

In all actuality specialized pointers won't consequently lead you to benefit, however they will do a ton of work for you. There are no questions that an able and experienced broker can accomplish benefit without markers, however they can at present help a great deal.

Actually, specialized pointers can accomplish a couple of brilliant things:

- show something that isn't self-evident;
- help to discover an exchange thought;
- save time for market investigation.

Each specialized pointer depends on a scientific equation. These equations make quick estimations of different value parameters and after that picture the outcome on the diagram. You don't have to compute anything yourself: simply go to MetaTrader menu, click on "Supplement" and afterward pick a marker you might want to add to the outline.

Simultaneously, specialized markers make their estimations just based on a value – the cash cites, which are reordered in the trading programming. Subsequently, pointers do have shaky areas: they can give signals which linger behind the cost (for instance, the cost has just fallen when the marker at long last gives a sign to sell).

Fortunately there are approaches to get a ton of advantages from specialized pointers. We will disclose how to do it in the passage that pursues.

The best specialized pointers for Forex brokers

Specialized markers are partitioned into a few gatherings relying upon their motivation. As motivations behind the markers are extraordinary, a dealer needs not one, yet a blend of a few pointers to open an exchange. In this article, we will tell about the 3 most prevalent specialized markers.

1. Moving Average – a pointer to recognize the pattern

Moving Average (MA) is a pattern marker. It recognizes and pursue the pattern.

Specialized standard: MA demonstrates a normal estimation of a cost over a picked timespan.

In straightforward terms: Moving Average pursues the cost. This line smooths the value unpredictability and dispose of the undesirable value "clamor", with the goal that you center around the primary pattern and not on revisions. It is important to comprehend that this pointer doesn't foresee the future cost, however, diagrams the present course of the market.

Favorable circumstances of Moving Average:

- identifies a bearing of a pattern;
- finds pattern inversions;
- shows potential help and obstruction levels.

Drawbacks of Moving Average:

- lags behind the present cost (will change more gradually than the value graph in light of the fact that the marker depends on the past costs).

Tips:

- There are 4 sorts of the Moving Averages – straightforward, exponential, direct weighted and smoothed. The contrast between them is only specialized (how much weight is allocated to the most recent information). We prescribe you to utilize Simple Moving Average as most brokers utilize this line.
- The most mainstream timeframes for MA are 200, 100, 50 and 20. 200-period MA may investigate a long haul "recorded" pattern, while the 20-time frame MA – to pursue a momentary pattern.

Step by step instructions to translate

To put it plainly, a pattern is bullish when the cost of a cash pair is over the MA and bearish – when the value falls beneath. Moreover, note how Moving Averages with various periods carry on towards one another.

Upward predisposition is affirmed when a shorter-term MA (for example 50-period) transcends the more extended term MA (for example 100-period). What's more, the other way around, a descending inclination is affirmed when a shorter-term MA goes underneath the more drawn out term MA.

End

Moving Average shows whether to purchase or sell a money pair (purchase in an upturn, sell in a downtrend). Mama won't let you know at what level to open your exchange (for that you'll require different markers). Therefore, applying a pattern pointer ought to be among the initial steps of your specialized investigation.

2. Bollinger Bands – a marker to gauge instability

Bollinger Bands estimates advertise instability (for example the level of variety of a trade cost).

Specialized standard: Bollinger Bands comprise of 3 lines. Each line (band) is a MA. The center band is normally a 20-period SMA. It recognizes pattern heading – simply like the MAs portrayed above do. Upper and lower groups (or "unpredictability" groups) are moved by two standard deviations above and beneath the center band.

In straightforward terms: Bollinger Bands pointer places the cost in a sort of box between the two outside lines. The cost is always rotating around the center line. It can proceed to test levels past the outside lines, however just for a brief timeframe and it won't have the option to escape. After such deviation from the inside, the cost should return back to the center. You can likewise see that during certain timeframes Bollinger lines come nearer together, while during different timeframes they spread and the range winds up more extensive. The smaller the range, the lower is showcase instability and, the other way around, the groups broaden when the market turns out to be progressively unstable.

Favorable circumstances of Bollinger Bands:

- The marker is really incredible in a sideways market (when a cash pair is exchanging a range). For this situation, the lines of the pointer can be utilized as help and obstruction levels, where dealers can open their positions.

Disservices of Bollinger Bands:

- During a solid pattern, the cost can spend quite a while at one Bollinger line and not go to the contrary one. Subsequently, we don't prescribe Bollinger Bands for drifting markets.

The most effective method to translate

The closer the value approaches the upper band, the more overbought the money pair moves toward becoming. Basically, at this point purchasers have just profited on the development of the cost and close their exchange to take benefit. The outcome is that the overbought pair quits rising and turns down. The value's ascent over the upper band might be a selling signal, while a decrease beneath the lower band – a purchasing signal.

The external groups naturally augment when instability increments and thin when unpredictability diminishes. High and low instability periods for the most part pursue one another, so the narrowing of the groups regularly implies that the unpredictability is going to increment pointedly.

Tips:

- We don't prescribe to utilize Bollinger Bands without affirmation from different pointers/specialized devices. Bollinger groups go well with candle designs, trendlines, and other value activities signals.

End

Bollinger Bands work best when the market isn't slanting. This marker can be an incredible reason for a trading framework, however, only it isn't sufficient: you'll have to utilize different instruments too.

3. MACD – a pointer that demonstrates the period of the market

MACD (Moving Average Convergence/Divergence) measures the main impetus behind the market. It indicates when the market becomes weary of moving one way and necessities a rest (revision).

Specialized standard: MACD histogram is the distinction between a 26-period and 12-period exponential moving midpoints (EMA). It additionally incorporates a sign line (9-period moving normal).

In straightforward terms: MACD depends on moving midpoints, yet it includes some different recipes also, so it has a place with a sort of specialized pointers known oscillators. Oscillators are appeared in independent boxes beneath the value outline. After an oscillator ascends to elevated levels, it needs to turn down. Normally so does the value diagram. The thing that matters is that while MACD needs to return near 0 or lower, the value's decrease will probably be littler. This is the manner by which MACD "predicts" the turns in cost.

Step by step instructions to translate

1. Dramatic Rise/Fall. Sell when histogram bars start declining after a major development. Purchase when histogram bars start becoming after a major decrease.
2. Crossovers between the histogram and the sign line can make showcase sections progressively exact. Purchase when the MACD-histogram transcends the

sign line. Sell when the MACD-histogram falls beneath the sign line.

3. Zero line as extra affirmation. When MACD crosses the zero line, it likewise demonstrates the quality of bulls or bears. Purchase when the MACD-histogram transcends 0. Sell when the MACD-histogram falls beneath 0. Note however, that such flag are more fragile than the past ones.

4. Divergence. In the event that a value rises and a MACD falls, it implies that the development of the cost isn't affirmed by the marker and the convention is going to end. Despite what might be expected, if a value falls and MACD rises, a bullish turn in the close term.

Tips

- Crossovers between the histogram and the sign line are the best sign from MACD.
- Hunt for divergences among MACD and the value: it's a decent sign of an up and coming revision.
- Favorable circumstances of MACD:
- MACD can be utilized both slanting and extending markets.
- If you comprehended MACD, it will be simple for you to figure out how different oscillators work: the standard is very comparative.
- Disservices of MACD:

- The marker falls behind the value graph, so a few sign arrive behind schedule and are not trailed by the solid move of the market.

End

It's great to have MACD on your diagram as it quantifies both pattern and energy. It very well may be a solid piece of an trading framework, in spite of the fact that we don't prescribe to settle on trading choices dependent on this pointer.

CHAPTER FOUR

FOREX REVERSAL TRADING

◆ ◆ ◆

An inversion is an adjustment in the value heading of a benefit. An inversion can strike the upside or drawback. Following an upturn, an inversion would be to the drawback. Following a downtrend, an inversion would be to the upside. Inversions depend on by and large value heading and are not ordinarily founded on a couple of periods/bars on a graph. Certain markers, such a moving normal or trendlines, may help in separating patterns just as spotting inversions.

KEY TAKEAWAYS

- An inversion demonstrates that the value bearing of an advantage has changed, from going up to going down, or from going down to going up.

- Traders attempt to escape places that are lined up with the pattern preceding an inversion, or they will get out once they see the inversion in progress.

- Reversals regularly allude to huge value changes, where the pattern alters course. Little counter-moves against the pattern are called pullbacks or unions.

- When it begins to happen, an inversion isn't discernable from a pullback. An inversion continues onward and structures another pattern, while a pullback finishes and after that the value starts moving back the slanting way.

What Does a Reversal Tell You?

Inversions regularly happen in intraday trading and happen rather rapidly, yet they likewise happen over days, weeks, and years. Inversions happen on various time spans which are significant to various brokers. An intraday inversion on a five-minute diagram doesn't make a difference to a long haul financial specialist who is looking for an inversion on every day or week by week graphs. However, the five-minute inversion is critical to an informal investor.

An upturn, which is a progression of higher swing highs and higher lows, turns around into a downtrend by changing to a progression of lower highs and lower lows. A downtrend, which is a progression of lower highs and lower lows, switches into an upturn by changing to a progression of higher highs and higher lows.

Patterns and inversions can be distinguished dependent on value activity alone, as depicted above, or different merchants incline toward the utilization of markers. Moving midpoints may help in spotting both the pattern and inversions. In the event that the cost is over a rising moving normal, at that point the pattern is up, yet when the value dips under the moving normal that could flag a potential value inversion.

Trendlines are likewise used to spot inversions. Since an upswing makes higher lows, a trendline can be drawn along those higher lows. At the point when the value dips under the trendline, that could show a pattern inversion.

In the event that inversions were anything but difficult to spot, and to separate from clamor or brief pullbacks, trading would be simple. Be that as it may, it isn't. In the case of utilizing value activity or markers, numerous bogus sign happen and some of the time inversions occur so rapidly that dealers aren't ready to act rapidly enough to maintain a strategic distance from an enormous misfortune.

Case of How to Use a Reversal

The graph demonstrates an upturn moving with a channel, making generally speaking higher highs and higher lows. The value first breaks out of the channel and underneath the trendline, flagging a conceivable pattern change. The value at that point likewise makes a lower low, dipping under the earlier low inside the channel. This further affirms the inversion to the drawback.

The value at that point proceeds with lower, making lower lows and lower highs. An inversion to the upside won't happen until the value makes a higher high and higher low. A move over the plunging trendline, however, could give an early cautioning indication of an inversion.

Alluding to the rising channel, the model likewise features the subjectivity of pattern investigation and inversions. A few times inside the channel the value makes a lower low comparative with an earlier swing, but the general direction stayed up.

Pattern FOLLOWING STRATEGY

Pattern following or pattern trading is a system in which one should purchase a benefit when its value pattern goes up, and sell when its pattern goes down, expecting value developments to continue.[1]

There are various methods, figurings and time allotments that might be utilized to decide the general heading of the market to produce an exchange signal (forex signals), including the present market value count, moving midpoints and channel breakouts. Dealers who utilize this procedure don't plan to conjecture or foresee explicit value levels; they just bounce on the pattern and ride it. Because of the various methods and time allotments utilized by pattern supporters to distinguish patterns, pattern adherents as a gathering are not in every case unequivocally related to each other.

Pattern-based trading is utilized by commodity trading advisors (CTAs) as the transcendent technique of specialized dealers. Research done by Galen Burghardt has demonstrated that between 2000-2009 there was an extremely high connection (.97) between pattern following CTAs and the more extensive CTA file

Moving Averages

Moving midpoints "smooth" value information by making a solitary streaming line. The line speaks to the normal cost over some undefined time frame. Which moving normal the dealer chooses to utilize is controlled when casing in which the individual exchanges. For speculators and long haul pattern supporters, the 200-day, 100-day and 50-day straightforward moving normal are prevalent decisions.

There are a few different ways to use the moving normal. The first is to take a gander at the point of the moving normal. On the off chance that it is generally moving on a level plane for an all-encompassing measure of time, at that point the cost isn't drifting, it is extending. On the off chance that the moving normal line is calculated up, an upturn is in progress. Moving midpoints don't anticipate however; they essentially show what the cost is doing, all things considered, over some stretch of time.

Hybrids are another approach to use moving midpoints. By plotting a 200-day and 50-day moving normal on your graph, a purchase sign happens when the 50-day crosses over the 200-day. A sell sign happens when the 50-day dips under the 200-day. The time periods can be adjusted to suit your individual trading time allotment.

At the point when the value crosses over a moving normal, it can likewise be utilized as a purchase signal, and when the value crosses beneath a moving normal, it very well may be utilized as a sell signal. Since cost is more unstable than the moving normal, this strategy is inclined to all the more false flag, as the diagram above shows.

Moving midpoints can likewise offer help or protection from the cost. The outline beneath demonstrates a 100-day moving normal going about as help (i.e., value ricochets off of it).

MACD (Moving Average Convergence Divergence)

The MACD is a wavering marker, fluctuating above and underneath zero. It is both a pattern following and force marker.

One essential MACD procedure is to see which side of zero the MACD lines are on in the histogram underneath the graph. Over zero for a continued timeframe, and the pattern is likely up; underneath zero for a supported timeframe, and the pattern is likely down. Potential purchase sign happen when the MACD moves over zero, and potential sell signals when it crosses beneath zero.

Sign line hybrids give extra purchase and sell signals. A MACD has two lines – a quick line and a moderate line. A purchase sign happens when the quick line crosses through or more the moderate line. A sell sign happens when the quick line crosses through and beneath the moderate line.

RED TO GREEN TRADING

Red green trading is the point at which a stock plunges beneath the earlier days close at that point moves back above. This red to green moves system is exceptionally well known in light of the fact that informal investors give specific consideration to these intraday moves.

Stock diagrams are a helpful method for survey the authentic value development of a security. The visual high points and low points of the line in the outline pass on importance such that a table loaded with numbers cannot. One snappy look at a diagram can give you important viewpoint on the stock's past presentation and fill in as a helpful information point in your investigation.

A commonplace line stock diagram in StockMarketEye resembles this:

The upper bit of the diagram is known as the Price graph. In the model over, the blue line demonstrates the end estimations of the stock. Moving the mouse over the graph will show the outline cursor. The subtleties of the day under the cursor are appeared in the top line of the graph region.

The lower bit of the graph is the trading Volume diagram. The taller the bar, the more volume there was on that day.

The hues in the Volume graph additionally have meaning. A green volume bar implies that the stock shut higher on that day stanzas the earlier day's nearby. A red volume bar implies that the stock shut lower on that day contrasted with the earlier day's nearby. A dark volume bar implies either that the stock shut at a similar value that day as it did the day preceding, or that the diagram doesn't have the earlier day's end cost to contrast and, (for example, in the principal volume bar in the graph).

Green and Red in the Price Chart

In the Price outline, both the Candlestick and Open-High-Low-Close (OHLC) diagram styles pass on additional significance when contrasted with a basic line graph. Rather than a solitary point (for example the end value), the day's action is appeared as an image, where the day's 4 information focuses (for example the open, high, low and shutting costs) are drawn.

The green and red renditions of the Candlestick and OHLC graph styles pass on additional significance through the hues. This equivalent significance is additionally obvious in the monochrome form of these diagram styles, yet a few financial specialists locate the green and red renditions assistance them to decipher the importance quicker.

The following graph demonstrates the "Candle Green/Red" stock outline type in real life. A green candle implies that the opening cost on that day was lower than the end value that day (for example the value climbed during the day); a red candle implies that the opening cost was higher than the end value that day (for example the value descended during the day).

Contrast that and the monochrome adaptation of a similar graph. A green candle is proportional to an open flame of the monochrome "Candle" graph type; a red candle is equal to a filled light.

At the point when the Colors contrast between the Price Chart and the Volume Chart

Albeit both the Price outline and Volume diagram can utilize green and red to pass on significance, the importance of the hues is marginally unique in every one of these graph types. Some of the time the candle or OHLC's shading will be not the same as the volume bar's shading.

For instance, if the stock completed higher than the earlier day, the volume bar will be green. Be that as it may, around the same time, if the stock moved lower from the opening value, the candle would be hued red.

This circumstance isn't that extraordinary. For instance, if there was a hole up at the open (as a result of positive organization news, examiner proposal, and so on), however the stock moved lower starting there for the duration of the day, yet remaining over the earlier day's end value, the candle would be hued red, yet the volume bar would be green.

Hues can be valuable to help pass on additional importance in stock outlines. Realizing how each shading is utilized in the various pieces of the stock outline will enable you to translate their importance quicker and get progressively out of the diagram.

SWING TRADING OR DAY TRADING?

Day Trading Versus Swing Trading: Potential Returns

Day trading pulls in dealers searching for fast aggravating of profits. Accept a broker dangers 0.5 percent of her capital on each exchange. In the event that she loses, she'll lose 0.5 percent, however on the off chance that she wins she'll make 1 percent (2:1 reward-to-risk proportion).

Likewise, accept she wins 50 percent of her exchanges. On the off chance that she makes six exchanges for every day, by and large, she will add about 1.5 percent to her account balance every day, less trading charges. Making even 1 percent daily would grow investment in excess of 200 percent through the span of the year, uncompounded.

On the other side, while the numbers appear to be anything but difficult to repeat for immense returns, nothing's ever that simple. Making twice as much on victors as you lost on washouts, while likewise winning 50 percent of the considerable number of exchanges you take, doesn't come effectively. You can make fast gains, yet you can likewise quickly drain your trading account through day trading.

Swing trading aggregates additions and misfortunes more gradually than day trading, however you can at present have certain swing exchanges that rapidly bring about huge increases or misfortunes. Accept a swing broker uses a similar risk the executives principle and dangers 0.5 percent of his capital on each exchange with an objective of attempting to make 1 percent to 2 percent on his triumphant exchanges.

Expect he procures 1.5 percent all things considered for winning exchanges, losing 0.5 percent on losing exchanges. He makes six exchanges for every month and wins 50 percent of those exchanges. In a normal month, the swing dealer could make 3 percent for him balance, less expenses. Through the span of the year, that turns out to around 36 percent, which sounds great however offers less potential than an informal investor's conceivable income.

These model situations serve to represent the differentiation between the two trading styles. Adjusting the level of exchanges won, the normal win contrasted with normal misfortune, or the quantity of exchanges, will definitely influence a system's acquiring potential.

When in doubt, day trading has more benefit potential, at any rate on smaller investments. As the size of the investment develops it ends up increasingly hard to viably use all the capital on transient day exchanges.

Informal investors may discover their rate returns decay the more capital they have. Their dollar returns may even now go up, since making 5 percent on $1 million likens to considerably more than 20 percent on $100,000. Swing merchants have less possibility of this occurrence.

Changing Capital Requirements

Capital prerequisites change as indicated by the market being traded on. Day trading and swing brokers can begin with contrasting measures of capital relying upon whether they exchange the stock, forex or prospects showcase.

Day trading stocks the US requires an account with $25,000. No lawful least exists to swing exchange stocks, albeit a swing broker will probably need to have at any rate $10,000 in their account, and ideally $20,000 if hoping to draw a pay from trading.

To day trade the forex showcase, no lawful least exists, however it is prescribed that brokers start with at any rate $500, yet ideally $1,000 or more. To swing exchange forex, the base suggested is about $1,500, yet ideally more. This measure of capital will enable you to enter at any rate a couple of exchanges one after another.

Day trading prospects, start with at any rate $5,000 to $7,500, and progressively capital would be far and away superior. These sums rely upon the prospects agreement being exchanged. Day trading a few agreements could require substantially more capital, while a couple of agreements, for example, smaller scale contracts, may require less.

To swing exchange an assortment of prospects contracts, you need at any rate $10,000, and likely $20,000 or more. The sum required relies upon the edge necessities of the particular agreement being exchanged.

Trading Times Differ

Both day trading and swing trading require time, yet day trading regularly occupies considerably more time. Informal investors for the most part exchange for at any rate two hours out of each day. Including planning time and outline/trading audit means spending in any event three to four hours at the PC, at least. On the off chance that an informal investor picks to exchange for in excess of a few hours per day, the time speculation goes up impressively and it turns into an all day work.

Swing trading, then again, can take substantially less time. For instance, in case you're swing trading daily, you could discover new exchanges and update arranges on current situations in around 45 minutes per night. These exercises may not be required on a daily premise.

Some swing dealers, taking exchanges that last weeks or months, may just need to search for exchanges and update arranges once per week, bringing the time duty down to about an hour out of every week rather than every night, or refreshing requests may not be required on a daily premise.

You should likewise do day trading while a market is open and dynamic. The best hours for day trading are restricted to specific times of the day. On the off chance that you can't day exchange during those hours, at that point pick swing trading as a superior choice. Swing dealers can search for exchanges or spot orders whenever of day, even after the market has shut.

Swing dealers are less influenced continuously to-second changes in the cost of an advantage. They center around the master plan, normally seeing every day graphs, so setting exchanges after the market closes on a specific day works fine and dandy. Informal investors make cash off second-by-second developments, so they should be included while the activity is occurring.

Center, Time and Practice

Swing trading and day trading both require a decent arrangement of work and information to create benefits reliably, in spite of the fact that the learning required isn't really "book smarts." Successful trading comes about because of finding a technique that delivers an edge, or a benefit over countless exchanges, and after that executing that methodology again and again.

Some learning available being exchanged and one beneficial procedure can begin creating salary, alongside parcels and heaps of training. Every day costs move uniquely in contrast to they did on the last, which means the dealer should have the option to execute his technique under different conditions and adjust as conditions change.

This shows a troublesome test, and predictable outcomes just originate from rehearsing a system under heaps of various market situations. That requires some serious energy and ought to include making several exchanges a demo account before gambling genuine capital.

Picking day trading or swing trading likewise comes down to character. Day trading regularly includes more pressure, requires continued concentration for broadened timeframes and takes inconceivable order. Individuals that like activity, have quick reflexes, or potentially like computer games and poker will in general incline toward day trading.

Swing trading occurs at a more slow pace, with any longer slips by between activities like entering or leaving trades. It can even now be high pressure, and furthermore requires gigantic order and tolerance.

It doesn't require as a lot of continued center, so in the event that you experience issues remaining centered, swing trading might be the better choice. Quick reflexes don't make a difference in swing trading as exchanges can be taken after the market closes and costs have quit moving.

Day trading and swing trading both offer opportunity the feeling that a dealer works for himself. Brokers ordinarily chip away at their own and answerable for subsidizing their investments and for all misfortunes and benefits created. One can contend that swing dealers have more opportunity as far as time since swing trading occupies less time than day exchanging.

A Final Comparison

One trading style isn't superior to the next; they simply suit varying needs. Day trading has more benefit potential, in any event in rate terms on littler estimated trading accounts. Swing merchants have a superior possibility of keeping up their rate returns even as their investment develops, in a specific way.

Capital necessities fluctuate a lot over the various markets and trading styles. Day trading requires additional time than swing trading, while both take a lot of training to pick up consistency. Day trading makes the best choice for the activity sweethearts. Those looking for a lower-stress and less time-serious choice can grasp swing trading.

Fundamental DAY TRADING STRATEGIES

5 Day Trading Strategies

1. Breakout

Breakout methodologies base on when the cost clears a predefined level on your graph, with expanded volume. The breakout dealer goes into a long position after the benefit or security breaks above opposition. Then again, you enter a short position once the stock breaks underneath help.

After a benefit or security exchanges past the predefined cost obstruction, instability generally increments and costs will frequently incline toward the breakout.

You have to locate the correct instrument to exchange. When doing this remember the advantage's help and obstruction levels. The more regularly the cost has hit these focuses, the more approved and significant they become.

Passage Points

This part is decent and clear. Costs set to close or more obstruction levels require a bearish position. Costs set to close and beneath a help level need a bullish position.

Plan your ways out

Utilize the advantage's ongoing presentation to set up a sensible value target. Utilizing diagram examples will make this procedure much progressively exact. You can figure the normal ongoing value swings to make an objective. In the event that the normal value swing has been 3 in the course of the last a few value swings, this would be a reasonable objective. When you've arrived at that objective you can leave the exchange and appreciate the benefit.

2. Scalping

One of the most famous systems is scalping. It's especially prominent in the forex market, and it hopes to profit by moment value changes. The main impetus is amount. You will hope to sell when the exchange winds up productive. This is a quick paced and energizing approach to exchange, however it very well may be dangerous. You need a high trading likelihood to try and out the generally safe versus remunerate proportion.

Be watchful for unstable instruments, appealing liquidity and be hot on timing. You can hardly wait for the market, you have to close losing exchanges as quickly as time permits.

3. Energy

Mainstream among trading procedures for learners, this methodology spins around following up on news sources and recognizing generous drifting moves with the help of high volume. There is consistently in any event one stock that moves around 20-30% every day, so there's adequate chance. You basically clutch your situation until you see indications of inversion and afterward get out.

On the other hand, you can blur the value drop. Along these lines round your value target is when volume begins to reduce.

This technique is basic and viable whenever utilized effectively. Be that as it may, you should guarantee you're mindful of up and coming news and income declarations. Only a couple of moments on each exchange will have a significant effect to your finish of day benefits.

4. Inversion

Albeit fervently discussed and possibly perilous when utilized by tenderfoots, invert trading is utilized everywhere throughout the world. It's otherwise called pattern trading, pull back slanting and a mean inversion system.

This system challenges essential rationale as you intend to exchange against the pattern. You should have the option to precisely recognize potential pullbacks, in addition to foresee their quality. To do this successfully you need top to bottom market information and experience.

The 'every day turn' technique is viewed as a one of a kind instance of switch trading, as it focuses on purchasing and selling the day by day low and high pullbacks/invert.

5. Utilizing Pivot Points

A day trading turn point system can be incredible for distinguishing and following up on basic help or potentially obstruction levels. It is especially helpful in the forex showcase. What's more, it very well may be utilized by range-bound merchants to recognize purposes of passage, while pattern and breakout dealers can utilize rotate focuses to find key levels that need to break for a transition to consider a breakout.

Figuring Pivot Points

A turn point is characterized as a point of pivot. You utilize the costs of the earlier day's high and low, in addition to the end cost of a security to compute the turn point.

Note that on the off chance that you figure a rotate point utilizing value data from a moderately brief time span, precision is frequently diminished.

Things being what they are, how would you ascertain a turn point?

- Central Pivot Point (P) = (High + Low + Close)/3

You would then be able to ascertain backing and opposition levels utilizing the rotate point. To do that you should utilize the accompanying recipes:

- First Resistance (R1) = (2*P) – Low
- First Support (S1) = (2*P) – High

The second degree of help and obstruction is then determined as pursues:

- Second Resistance (R2) = P + (R1-S1)
- Second Support (S2) = P – (R1-S1)

Application

At the point when applied to the FX advertise, for instance, you will discover the trade range for the session frequently happens between the turn point and the principal backing and opposition levels. This is on the grounds that a high number of brokers play this range.

It's additionally important, this is one of the frameworks and strategies that can be applied to accounts as well. For instance, it can help structure a compelling S&P day trading procedure.

Farthest point Your Losses

This is especially significant in case you're utilizing edge. Prerequisites for which are generally high for informal investors. At the point when you exchange on edge you are progressively helpless against sharp value developments. Indeed, this implies the potential for more noteworthy benefit, yet it likewise implies the probability of critical misfortunes. Luckily, you can utilize stop-misfortunes.

The stop-misfortune controls your risk for you. In a short position, you can put a stop-misfortune over an ongoing high, for long positions you can put it underneath an ongoing low. You can likewise make it dependent on instability.

For instance, a stock value moves by £0.05 every moment, so you place a prevent misfortune £0.15 away from your entrance request, enabling it to swing (ideally in the normal course).

One prominent methodology is to set up two stop-misfortunes. Initially, you put in a physical stop-misfortune request at a particular value level. This will be the most capital you can stand to lose. Besides, you make a psychological stop-misfortune. Spot this at the point your entrance criteria are ruptured. So if the exchange makes an unforeseen turn, you'll make a quick exit.

Forex Trading Strategies

Forex procedures are risk commonly as you have to amass your benefits in a short space of time. You can apply any of the techniques above to the forex market, or you can see our forex page for nitty gritty system models.

Digital money Trading Strategies

The energizing and eccentric digital currency market offers a lot of chances for the turned on informal investor. You don't have to comprehend the perplexing specialized cosmetics of bitcoin or ethereum, nor do you have to hold a long haul see on their feasibility. Just utilize clear procedures to benefit from this unpredictable market.

To discover cryptographic money explicit systems, visit our digital currency page.

Stock Trading Strategies

Day trading methodologies for stocks depend on a considerable lot of similar standards plot all through this page, and you can utilize a significant number of the techniques sketched out above. Beneath however is a particular technique you can apply to the financial exchange.

Moving Average Crossover

You will require three moving normal lines:

- One set at 20 periods – This is your quick moving normal
- One set at 60 periods – This is your moderate moving normal
- One set at 100 periods – This is your pattern marker

This is one of the moving midpoints techniques that produces a purchase signal when the quick moving normal traverses the moderate moving normal. A sell sign is created just when the quick moving normal crosses beneath the moderate moving normal.

In this way, You'll open a position when the moving normal line crosses a single way and you'll close the position when it crosses back the contrary way.

How might you set up there's very a pattern? You realize the pattern is on if the value bar remains above or underneath the 100-time frame line.

For more data on stocks procedures, see our Stocks and offers page.

Spread Betting Strategies

Spread wagering enables you to theorize on a colossal number of worldwide markets without ever really owning the benefit. In addition, methodologies are generally direct.

On the off chance that you might want to see the absolute greatest day trading systems uncovered, see our spread wagering page.

CFD Strategies

Building up a powerful day trading technique can be convoluted. Be that as it may, choose an instrument, for example, a CFD and your activity might be to some degree simpler.

CFDs are worried about the distinction between where an exchange is entered and exit. Late years have seen their prevalence flood. This is on the grounds that you can benefit when the fundamental resource moves in connection to the position taken, while never owning the basic resource.

For CFD explicit day trading tips and methodologies, see our CFD page.

Territorial Differences

Various markets accompany various chances and obstacles to survive. Day trading systems for the Indian market may not be as powerful when you apply them in Australia. For instance, a few nations might doubt of the news, so the market may not respond similarly as you'd anticipate that them should back home.

Guidelines are another factor to consider. Indian methodologies might be customized to fit inside explicit guidelines, for example, high least value adjusts in edge accounts. In this way, get on the web and check cloud guidelines won't affect your methodology before you put your well-deserved cash on hold.

You may likewise discover various nations have diverse expense provisos to hop through. In case you're situated in the West however need to apply your typical day trading procedures the Philippines, you have to get your work done first.

What sort of assessment will you need to pay? Will you need to pay it abroad as well as locally? Minor assessment dissimilarities could have a critical effect to your finish of day benefits.

Risk Management

Stop-misfortune

Techniques that work consider. On the off chance that you don't oversee chance, you'll lose beyond what you can bear the cost of and be out of the game before you know it. This is the reason you ought to consistently use a stop-misfortune.

The cost may resemble it's moving toward the path you trusted, however it could turn around whenever. A stop-misfortune will control that risk. You'll leave the exchange and possibly cause an insignificant misfortune if the benefit or security doesn't come through.

Keen merchants don't as a rule, risk over 1% of their account balance on a solitary exchange. So on the off chance that you have £27,500 in your account, you can risk up to £275 per exchange.

Position size

It will likewise empower you to choose the ideal position size. Position size is the quantity of offers taken on a solitary exchange. Take the distinction between your entrance and stop-misfortune costs. For instance, on the off chance that your entrance point is £12 and your stop-misfortune is £11.80, at that point your risk is £0.20 per share.

Presently to make sense of what number of exchanges you can take on a solitary exchange, partition £275 by £0.20. You can take a position size of up to 1,375 offers. That is the greatest position you could take to adhere to your 1% risk point of confinement.

Likewise, check there is adequate volume in the stock/advantage for ingest the position size you use. Likewise, remember that in the event that you take a position size too enormous for the market, you could experience slippage on your entrance and stop-misfortune.

CHAPTER FIVE

BASIC FOREX TRADING STRATEGY

◆ ◆ ◆

Swing trading systems #1: Stuck in a crate
What's more, a certain something…

The swing trading systems I'm going to impart to have "fascinating" names appended to it.

This encourages you comprehend the trading arrangement better so you realize how to apply it to your trading.

Presently, let me acquaint with you the principal swing trading procedure for now…

Stuck in a crate.

It's swing trading a range showcase in light of the fact that the market is "trapped" among Support and Resistance (fairly like a container).

Here's the means by which it works:

1. Identify a range showcase
2. Wait at the cost to break beneath Support
3. If the value breaks beneath Support, at that point hang tight at a solid cost dismissal (a nearby above Support)
4. If there's a solid value dismissal, at that point go long on the following light open
5. Set your stop misfortune 1 ATR beneath the flame low and take benefits before Resistance

Here's a model:

Presently you may ponder:

"For what reason would it be a good idea for me to take benefits before Resistance?"

Review...

As a swing broker, you're searching for "one move" in the market.

So to guarantee a high likelihood of accomplishment, you need to leave your exchanges before the selling weight steps in (which is at Resistance).

Swing trading systems #2: Catch the wave

This swing trading system centers around getting "one move" in a slanting business sector (like a surfer attempting to get the wave).

The thought here is to enter after the pullback has finished when the pattern is probably going to proceed.

Be that as it may...

This doesn't work for a wide range of patterns.

Rather, you need to exchange slants that have a more profound pullback in light of the fact that there's more "meat" towards the upside.

As a rule, you need to see a pullback at any rate towards the 50-time frame moving normal (MA) or more profound.

Presently, how about we figure out how to get the wave with this swing trading procedure...

1. Identify a pattern that regards the 50MA
2. If the market approaches the moving normal, at that point sit tight at a bullish cost dismissal
3. If there's a bullish value dismissal, at that point go long on next light
4. Set your stop misfortune 1 ATR beneath the low and take benefits just before the swing high

Here's a model:

Do you need more models?

At that point go watch this preparation video where I'll tell you the best way to distinguish this swing trading arrangement bit by bit...

Presently you may ponder:

"Be that as it may, why the 50-time frame moving normal?"

I go with the 50MA on the grounds that it's viewed by dealers around the globe so that could prompt an inevitable outcome.

Also, for the most part, the 50MA agrees with past Resistance turned Support which makes it progressively noteworthy.

Presently, it doesn't mean you can't utilize 55, 67, 89, or whatever moving normal you pick in light of the fact that the idea is what makes a difference.

Swing trading procedures #3: Fade the move

Presently you're presumably thinking:

"What's the importance of blur?"

It implies... to conflict with.

Essentially, you're trading against the force (otherwise called counter-pattern).

Along these lines, in the event that you're the broker that likes to "conflict with the group", at that point this trading procedure is for you.

Here's the means by which it works...

1. Identify a solid energy move into Resistance that takes out the past high
2. Look at a solid cost dismissal as the flame frames a solid bearish close
3. Go short on the following flame and set your stop misfortune 1 ATR over the highs
4. Take benefits before the closest swing low

Instructions to deal with your exchanges so you can exchange with certainty and conviction

Presently with exchange the executives, there are 2 different ways you can go about it...

1. Passive exchange the executives
2. Active administration

I'll clarify...

1. Uninvolved exchange the executives

For this strategy, you'll either let the market either hit your stop misfortune or target benefit — anything between, you'll sit idle.

In a perfect world, you need to set your prevent misfortune away from the "clamor" of the business sectors and have an objective benefit inside sensible reach (before key market structure).

Here are the experts and cons of it...

Experts:

- Trading is progressively loose as your choices become increasingly "computerized"

Cons:

- You can't leave your exchange early despite the fact that the market is giving indications of inversion
- Possible to see a triumphant exchange become a full 1R misfortune

2. Dynamic administration

For this, you'll observe how the market responds and after that choose whether you need to hold or leave the exchange.

Presently, this is significant...

For a functioning way to deal with work, you should deal with your exchanges on your entrance time span (or higher).

Try not to wrongly manage it on a lower time span since you'll unnerve yourself out of an exchange on each pullback that happens.

Here are the geniuses and cons of it...

Aces:

- You can limit your misfortunes as opposed to getting a full 1R misfortune

Cons:

- More upsetting
- You may leave your exchange too early without giving it enough space to run

In the event that dynamic exchange the executives is for you, at that point here are two procedures you can consider:

- Moving normal
- Previous bar high/low

Allow me to clarify...

Moving Average

This system includes utilizing a moving normal marker to trail your stops.

You'll clutch the exchange if the cost doesn't break past the moving normal.

In the event that it does, at that point you'll leave the exchange.

A model:

This strategy is helpful for swing trading systems like Catch the Wave in light of the fact that the moving normal will in general go about as a unique Support and Resistance in drifting markets.

Past bar high/low

This procedure depends on the past bar high/low to trail your stop misfortune.

This implies on the off chance that you're short, at that point you'll trail your stop misfortune utilizing the past bar high.

On the off chance that the market breaks and closes above it, at that point you'll leave the exchange (and the other way around).

This is what I mean:

This procedure is helpful for swing trading systems like Fade the Move on the grounds that the market can rapidly switch against you.

In this way, you would prefer not to give your exchange an excess of space to move around and immediately cut your misfortunes when the market give indications of inversion.

ADVANCED FOREX TRADING STRATEGIES

Swing trading enables you to profit when the market is bullish, or bearish, or simply going sideways. That is the reason it has an unmistakable preferred position over different ways to deal with contributing. The objective is to profit, not to lay one's expectations on the eventual fate of a stock, a part, or the economy.

What is Swing Trading Everyone knows about waves. A wave interchanges from positive to negative, at that point to positive and negative, etc. Waves are found in nature – you see waves when you toss a stone into a lake. Sound is transmitted in waves. Also, when stock costs change, they pursue a wave-like example. The wave is once in a while as methodical a sine wave, however they are waves in any case, and we utilize these waves in Swing Trading.

How about we Look at an Up Trends

The graph underneath demonstrates the value development of Myriad Genetics (MYGN) in an upturn. Notice that after the value climbs, it takes a rest, or pulls back. At the point when we swing exchange an upswing, we purchase on the draw back. An upswing can be recognized by a progression of higher highs and higher lows (the base of each draw back). As it were, an upswing is a progression of progressive meetings with each rally going higher than the past one and each draw back halting over the past one. The value development looks increasingly like the crisscross of a saw cutting edge than a sinusoid, however once an upturn is built up the example will in general recurrent itself. In swing trading we benefit from the consistency of the example. We purchase during the dismantle back to build our odds of making a benefit.

We should Look at a Down Trend The outline beneath demonstrates the value development of Verisign (VRSN) in a downtrend. Notice that after the value descends, it takes a rest, or pulls up. The value development pursues a crisscross example. A downtrend can be distinguished by a progression of lower lows and lower highs (the pinnacle of each draw up). At the point when we swing exchange a downtrend, we undercut during a draw up. In the event that you are new to undercutting, we talk about it in the following session.

The Steps in Swing Trading

Initially, confine your determination to the universe of stocks that satisfy certain criteria.

Pick stocks that …

- Have a cost of at any rate $7
- Have a normal day by day volume of at any rate 500,000 offers

At that point …

Stage 1 – Identify a stock that is in an upturn or a downtrend.

Stage 2 – For stocks in an upturn, distinguish those that are encountering a draw back. For stocks in a downtrend, distinguish those that are encountering a draw up.

Stage 3 – Once a proper up-and-comer is distinguished, submit a limit request to purchase (upswing) or undercut (downtrend) the stock dependent on the Master Plan.

Stage 4 – Once a stock has been exchanged (a position opened), put in a stop-misfortune request to constrain drawback risk and put in a limit request to recognize the cost at which you will take benefits

Stage 5 – At the finish of every day, modify the stop misfortune costs dependent on the Master Plan.

4.5 What Can You Expect?

First – just a segment of your exchanges will be executed. The Master Plan is intended to just exchange stocks that at first move the foreseen way. In the event that the value moves the other way (keeps pulling back or pulling up), the exchange isn't set.

Second – you will hold positions for a constrained measure of time. While swing trading isn't day trading, you are just holding situations until targets are met.

Third – a portion of your exchanges will bring about misfortunes, anyway misfortunes are limited by the Master Plan which raises the stops as the stock value rises; this is known as trailing stops. Being taught, and following the Master Plan will safeguard that benefits surpass misfortunes which means you will profit.

4.6 How Do You Identify Stocks that are Appropriate for Swing Trading?

The majority of the techniques that are utilized to distinguish stocks that are fitting for swing trading depend on specialized investigation. Specialized examination is a method for utilizing authentic value/volume examples to foresee future conduct. It isn't important to have a nitty gritty comprehension of specialized investigation so as to swing exchange. There are devices accessible that can help speculators at each level – from beginner to master.

Examples of overcoming adversity

George Soros

If we somehow happened to ask, "Who is the best forex dealer?" Soros' name would positively consistently figure high on any rundown. Mr Soros is known as perhaps the best speculator ever. He fixed his notoriety for being an amazing cash director by supposedly benefitting more than £1 billion from his short position in pound sterling. He broadly did as such in front of Black Wednesday, 16 September 1992.

He once told the Wall Street Journal "I'm rich since I realize when I'm off-base". This statement shows the two his readiness to cut an exchange that isn't working, and the significant level of order that is shared by the best Forex brokers. So George Soros is number 1 on our rundown as presumably a standout amongst other known 'world's best Forex merchants', and surely one of the globe's most noteworthy workers from a momentary exchange

Stanley Druckenmiller

George Soros throws a long shadow. what's more, it shouldn't come as an over the top astonishment that this effective Forex dealer has connections to the following broker on our rundown. Stanley Druckenmiller considers George Soros his tutor. Truth be told, Mr.

Druckenmiller worked close by him at the Quantum Fund for over 10 years. In any case, Druckenmiller has set up an imposing notoriety in his very own right, effectively overseeing billions of dollars for his own store, Duquesne Capital. He can without much of a stretch be considered as outstanding amongst other informal investors on the planet.

Just as being a piece of Soros' well known Black Wednesday exchange, Mr Druckenmiller bragged an extraordinary investment progressive long stretches of twofold digit gains with Duquesne, before his possible retirement. Druckenmiller's total assets is esteemed at more than $2 billion. Druckenmiller says that his trading reasoning for structure long haul returns spins around safeguarding capital, and after that forcefully seeking after benefits when exchanges are going great. This methodology makes light of the significance of being correct or wrong.

Rather, it stresses the benefit of boosting the open door when you are correct and limiting the harm when you are incorrect. As Druckenmiller expressed when met for the praised book 'The New Market Wizards', "there are a great deal of shoes on the rack; wear just the ones that fit."

Bill Lipschutz

Bill Lipschutz made benefits of a huge number of dollars at the FX branch of Salomon Brothers during the 1980s - regardless of no past experience of the money markets. Frequently called the Sultan of Currencies, Mr Lipschutz portrays FX as an extremely mental market. What's more, similar to our other fruitful Forex dealers, the Sultan accepts showcase discernments help decide value activity as much as unadulterated essentials.

Here's some of Lipschutz other key fundamentals.

- Any trading thought should be all around contemplated before you place the trade
- Build a situation as the market goes your direction and leave a similar way
- Start to straightforwardness up once there are signs that the basics and the value activity are starting to change
- There is a should know about the market's core interest
- FX is a 24-hour showcase, and doesn't quit moving when you head to sleep

Lipschutz additionally focuses on the need to oversee risk, saying that your trade size ought to be picked to abstain from being constrained out of your position, if your planning is estimated.

Swing trading enables you to profit when the market is bullish, or bearish, or simply going sideways. That is the reason it has a particular bit of leeway over different ways to deal with contributing. The objective is to profit, not to lay one's expectations on the fate of a stock, a division, or the economy.

What is Swing Trading Everyone knows about waves. A wave interchanges from positive to negative, at that point to positive and negative, etc. Waves are found in nature – you see waves when you toss a stone into a lake. Sound is transmitted in waves. Also, when stock costs change, they pursue a wave-like example. The wave is once in a while as methodical a sine wave, however they are waves all things considered, and we utilize these waves in Swing Trading.

How about we Look at an Up Trends

The outline underneath demonstrates the value development of Myriad Genetics (MYGN) in an upswing. Notice that after the value climbs, it takes a rest, or pulls back. At the point when we swing exchange an upturn, we purchase on the draw back. An upswing can be recognized by a progression of higher highs and higher lows (the base of each draw back). At the end of the day, an upturn is a progression of progressive meetings with each rally going higher than the past one and each draw back halting over the past one. The value development looks progressively like the crisscross of a saw cutting edge than a sinusoid, yet once an upswing is set up the example will in general recurrent itself. In swing trading we benefit from the consistency of the example. We purchase during the destroy back to build our odds of making a benefit.

How about we Look at a Down Trend The graph underneath demonstrates the value development of Verisign (VRSN) in a downtrend. Notice that after the value descends, it takes a rest, or pulls up. The value development pursues a crisscross example. A downtrend can be distinguished by a progression of lower lows and lower highs (the pinnacle of each draw up). At the point when we swing exchange a downtrend, we undercut during a draw up. In the event that you are new to undercutting, we examine it in the following session.

The Steps in Swing Trading

To begin with, limit your determination to the universe of stocks that satisfy certain criteria.

Pick stocks that …

- Have a cost of in any event $7
- Have a normal every day volume of at any rate 500,000 offers

At that point ...

Stage 1 – Identify a stock that is in an upswing or a downtrend.

Stage 2 – For stocks in an upswing, recognize those that are encountering a draw back. For stocks in a downtrend, distinguish those that are encountering a draw up.

Stage 3 – Once a fitting applicant is distinguished, put in a limit request to purchase (upturn) or undercut (downtrend) the stock dependent on the Master Plan.

Stage 4 – Once a stock has been exchanged (a position opened), put in a stop-misfortune request to restrain drawback risk and submit a limit request to distinguish the cost at which you will take benefits

Stage 5 – At the finish of every day, change the stop misfortune costs dependent on the Master Plan.

4.5 What Can You Expect?

First – just a segment of your exchanges will be executed. The Master Plan is intended to just exchange stocks that at first move the foreseen way. On the off chance that the value moves the other way (keeps pulling back or pulling up), the exchange isn't set.

Second – you will hold positions for a constrained measure of time. While swing trading isn't day trading, you are just holding situations until targets are met.

Third – a portion of your exchanges will bring about misfortunes, anyway misfortunes are limited by the Master Plan which raises the stops as the stock value rises; this is known as trailing stops. Being taught, and following the Master Plan will protect that benefits surpass misfortunes which means you will profit.

4.6 How Do You Identify Stocks that are Appropriate for Swing Trading? The majority of the strategies that are utilized to distinguish stocks that are fitting for swing exchanging depend on specialized investigation. Specialized investigation is a method for utilizing invested value/volume examples to anticipate future conduct. It isn't important to have a point by point comprehension of specialized examination so as to swing exchange. There are instruments accessible that can help speculators at each level – from tenderfoot to master.

Examples of overcoming adversity

George Soros

If we somehow managed to ask, "Who is the best forex dealer? " Soros' name would surely consistently figure high on any rundown. Mr Soros is known as perhaps the best financial specialist ever. He fixed his notoriety for being an incredible cash director by purportedly benefitting more than £1 billion from his short position in pound sterling. He broadly did as such in front of Black Wednesday, 16 September 1992.

He once told the Wall Street Journal "I'm rich since I realize when I'm off-base". This statement shows the two his eagerness to cut an exchange that isn't working, and the elevated level of order that is shared by the best Forex dealers. So George Soros is number 1 on our rundown as likely extraordinary compared to other known 'world's best Forex dealers', and surely one of the globe's most elevated workers from a momentary exchange

Stanley Druckenmiller

George Soros throws a long shadow. also, it shouldn't come as an over the top amazement that this effective Forex broker has connections to the following merchant on our rundown. Stanley Druckenmiller considers George Soros his guide. Indeed, Mr. Druckenmiller worked close by him at the Quantum Fund for over 10 years. Be that as it may, Druckenmiller has built up a considerable notoriety in his very own right, effectively overseeing billions of dollars for his very own reserve, Duquesne Capital. He can without much of a stretch be considered as a standout amongst other informal investors on the planet.

Just as being a piece of Soros' renowned Black Wednesday exchange, Mr Druckenmiller bragged a mind blowing investment progressive long stretches of twofold digit gains with Duquesne, before his possible retirement. Druckenmiller's total assets is esteemed at more than $2 billion. Druckenmiller says that his exchanging reasoning for structure long haul returns spins around protecting capital, and after that forcefully seeking after benefits when exchanges are going great. This methodology makes light of the significance of being correct or wrong.

Rather, it stresses the benefit of boosting the open door when you are correct and limiting the harm when you are incorrect. As Druckenmiller expressed when met for the praised book 'The New Market Wizards', "there are a great deal of shoes on the rack; wear just the ones that fit."

Bill Lipschutz

Bill Lipschutz made benefits of a huge number of dollars at the FX branch of Salomon Brothers during the 1980s - regardless of no past experience of the money markets. Frequently called the Sultan of Currencies, Mr Lipschutz portrays FX as an exceptionally mental market. Also, similar to our other effective Forex brokers, the Sultan accepts advertise discernments help decide value activity as much as unadulterated basics.

Here's some of Lipschutz other key principles.

- Any exchanging thought should be very much contemplated before you place the exchange
- Build a situation as the market goes your direction and leave a similar way
- Start to simplicity up once there are signs that the basics and the value activity are starting to change
- There is a should know about the market's core interest
- FX is a 24-hour showcase, and doesn't quit moving when you head to sleep

COMMON OBSTACLES AND MISTAKES

Starting brokers regularly face difficult occasions when beginning to exchange. Regardless of whether they exchange on a live or demo account, the challenges looked by changed new dealers are regularly the equivalent. I've made a rundown of the 5 regular challenges in exchanging looked by those beginning.

One thing you should know, I experienced every one of them.

1) Confusion About What To Trade

As brokers, there is a colossal distinction between what we realize and what we truly need to know. That is the reason disarray is a piece of the troubles in exchanging.

For a few, the trouble is getting overpowered by data on Forex, trading procedures, brain science, chance administration strategies, etc.

Following that, those brokers can't make a difference anything since they don't have a clue where to begin. I've been in this circumstance. As a straightforward model, you can find out about graph examples trading, inversion methodologies, pattern following procedures and scalping.

At that point, what do you exchange?...

A typical normal for effective merchants, which I got from the book Millionaire Traders, is that some may exchange the other way to one another. Notwithstanding, their prosperity has been made by choosing one approach to exchange and adhering to it.

Therefore, I put stock in turning into the "master" of your own style. No single trading style is superior to other people. What has the effect is the individual behind it.

For other people, the issue is that they are not learning the correct things. You can learn as much as you need however as long as you don't realize what you have to realize, no good thing will occur.

That is the reason it is essential to comprehend what you should realize before beginning to exchange. While trading is an order where you consistently learn, I have confidence in starting with exactly what you need and expanding on it.

I likewise know individuals who don't adapt enough. They start, as I did, with zero information and that is likewise an issue. Obviously, you can learn in transit yet that makes things considerably more disappointing and troublesome.

To put it plainly, get instructed by learning the correct things and you'll defeat the first of your challenges in exchanging.

2) No Confidence

How frequently do I hear, "among my challenges in trading is creating certainty!"

The appropriate response is: consistently.

This parts intently identifies with trading convictions. Not exclusively should you be certain you realize your methodology works, you must be positive about your capacity to prevail as a merchant.

Regardless of how hard you attempt to persuade yourself that your system and technique are working, there's just a single method to develop your certainty about them. You need to test and trial.

I'm not catching that's meaning? It implies you should:

- 1) Backtest your trading system and guarantee it gives a satisfactory return
- 2) Experiment with your way of life and propensities to see whether they amplify your exhibition

On the off chance that you've accomplished those two things and still battle in trading, it implies you need to uncover further and look your own convictions' effect on your trading. You should guarantee that they set you up for progress. If not, try to get the correct convictions.

3) Getting Stuck In A Circle

I've been there for quite a while…

What I mean by stalling out around is accomplishing the terrible things again and again. That can occur in two different ways:

- 1) Constant quest for data
- 2) Repeating a similar trading botch

Steady quest for data

With all the data today, it is so natural to fall into a hover of "scan for data'. That is ordinary There's really a logical purpose for that. As per inquire about, dopamine makes us look for stuff. When we've discovered something, narcotic prizes us by giving a sentiment of joy. The issue here is that we fall into a circle.

When we see that our trading procedure isn't immaculate, we start scanning for another one, until we locate the following "best one". We at that point feel better yet just for a brief timeframe.

At the point when a couple more misfortunes happen, the procedure re-begins. Susan Weinschenk, Phd, has composed an extraordinary article titled Dopamine Makes You Addicted To Seeking Information. I unquestionably suggest watching that!

I unquestionably suggest watching that!

Rehashing a similar trade botch

The second method for being stuck around concerns botches we make in trading. Presently, get that, as a fledgling, it is absolutely typical and even fundamental to commit errors when you exchange.

The key lies in not rehashing those slip-ups again and again.

The best arrangement and the one I use all things considered is to keep a diary of your errors. It doesn't need to be exceptionally unpredictable nor it ought to be. Just record visual cues of your missteps.

In the event that you've just done that, amazing! Be that as it may, you've just applied portion of the arrangement. The following activity is to survey your missteps occasionally. I audit my diary consistently.

I found that utilizing a paper diary to record my errors made it simpler to recall them.

4) Taking Improper Action In A Trade

One of the main considerations in my misfortunes as an apprentice in trading was not carrying on appropriately once I took my exchanges. I could as a rule, with certain special cases, enter the exchange as a star. In any case, when I was in the exchange, things began getting awful...

What I mean by acting inappropriately:

- 1) Closing an exchange too soon
- 2) Not securing benefit
- 3) Not putting a stop misfortune
- 4) Moving a stop misfortune

Obviously, there are much progressively inappropriate practices once you've entered an exchange. That will rely upon your trading methodology.

As referenced already, keeping a diary of your slip-ups when they happen is a key conduct to have in the event that you need to abstain from rehashing your slip-ups again and again.

All challenges in trading can be handled, however you should initially know that you experience them.

Something else that worked for me and numerous others in trading is contemplation. Presently, the best individual I know to discuss is Yvan Byeajee, He shares his reflection practice in scene 7 of the Desire To Trade Podcast.

Whatever you may consider reflection, inquire about has demonstrated that there are advantages to it. Contemplation is known to quiet your brain at the time and help you in unpleasant circumstances.

I certainly suggest attempting it. I began utilizing Headspace, an application that aides you through brief times of reflection.

5) Having Improper Expectations

I heard something that stalled out in my brain as of late:

AS A BEGINNER, YOU SHOULD NOT HAVE THE RIGHT TO EXPECT ANYTHING.

One of the visitor on the Desire To Trade Podcast (Episode 2), Houston Truong, talked about this thought in an article titled You're Getting The Results You're Supposed To Get.

How obvious is that? All things considered, it truly is.

It is totally improper for merchants simply beginning to anticipate a specific cash result. The main thing you need to do when beginning to exchange is applying your methodology. That is it. At that point, see what you get and perceive how you can improve later on.

I've seen that a few brokers set the bar too high that makes it harder for them to focus on trading. They become progressively avaricious and neglect to execute their arrangement.

As it were, don't be discouraged on the off chance that you don't double your investment in the first year of live trading. Trade and you'll get whatever you get.

In the event that you do that, you are superior to most merchants (the 68% who lost cash in every one of the previous 4 quarters in 2014 as indicated by Bloomberg) in light of the fact that you're less inclined to encounter avarice and disappointment, and bound to get results.

CHAPTER SIX

WHAT IS PONZI AND HOW TO AVOID

◆ ◆ ◆

Ponzi is a type of misrepresentation that draws financial specialists and pays benefits to prior speculators with assets from later financial specialists. The plan persuades that benefits arc originating from item deals or different methods, and they stay uninformed that different speculators are the wellspring of assets. A Ponzi plan can keep up the dream of a reasonable business as long as new financial specialists contribute new assets, and as long as the vast majority of the speculators don't request full reimbursement and still have faith in the non-existent resources they are implied to claim.

MAGINE TRUSTING YOUR well-deserved cash, for example, your retirement investment funds—to a money related counsel just to lose it all in a fake plan. Fixating on whether your cash director could be the following Bernard Madoff, the supposed driving force of a $50 billion Ponzi plot, won't do a lot of good, yet some solid distrust won't hurt. Here are five hints for financial specialists so they can abstain from getting swindled:

Ensure your counselor is genuine. In case you're searching for a guide, approach companions and relatives for suggestions—yet don't stop there. A startling truth is that anybody can consider oneself a monetary organizer or counselor, so it pays to check with national associations that issue qualifications. They incorporate the National Association of Personal Financial Advisers, the Financial Planning Association, and the Certified Financial Board of Standards. Every offer an accessible database with contact data for organizers in each state. The American Institute of Certified Public Accountants has a rundown of CPAs who've earned the individual money related pro assignment.

Burrow profound. Put on your gumshoes and discover to what extent the counselor has been in the business. Request to see their ADV Form, Part II, which an organizer documents with the Securities and Exchange Commission. It contains data about the guide's experience, administrations, and expenses. Check for grievances documented however your state's protections controller (contact data is accessible here). A site visit may likewise be useful, says Tim Kochis, CEO of Aspiriant, a riches the executives firm with workplaces in San Francisco and Los Angeles that takes into account high-total assets customers. "Notoriety and clear reputation are insufficient," he says. "You need to go path past that to truly explore the tasks of the organization and see whether what is asserted is genuine."

Comprehend the contrast between a supervisor and an overseer. A caretaker, which would incorporate the Fidelitys and Charles Schwabs of the world, is in control of your venture account and issues intermittent explanations of exchanges. The chief of advantages executes those exchanges. "Many individuals neglect to comprehend why it's essential to isolate these capacities," says Kochis. "Cheats quite often happen when those two things are assembled." at the end of the day, pay special mind to a speculation supervisor who needs unlimited oversight of your cash and asks that looks at be made to the person in question. You can rest tight if your assets are in the care of a representative vendor firm controlled by the Financial Industry Regulatory Authority and supported by the Securities Investor Protection Corp. In any case, ensure you get in any event quarterly articulations, says Mickey Cargile, author and overseeing accomplice WNB Private Client Services, which is situated in Midland, Texas. "The key is that you get it legitimately from the caretaker and not from the counsel."

Be suspicious of pitches for fascinating or cloud items. Banks, businesses, and organizers offer a wide scope of money related items, including intriguing ventures that fuse influence and complex subordinates. In the event that you get a pitch for a benefit class you're inexperienced with, ensure you comprehend the procedure by which it accomplishes returns. Jim Wiandt, editorial manager and distributer of the Journal of Indexes and distributer of IndexUniverse.com, puts it like this: "On the off chance that you don't get it, you shouldn't be in it." Cargile makes it a stride further: "Just put resources into straightforward resources. We don't put resources into anything we can't go to trade out three days or less, which limits us to stocks, securities, common assets, and trade exchanged assets." A flexible investments, which isn't required to reveal its property, is a case of a nontransparent venture. Likewise, be particularly attentive if your guide makes light of or denies chance.

Be particularly cautious in case you're nearing or in retirement. As per an ongoing report by the North American Securities Administrators Association, about portion of all financial specialist grievances submitted to state protections organizations originated from the senior set. As indicated by the affiliation, fake administrators some of the time con more established financial specialists through free-lunch classes that are trailed by calls from sales reps a couple of days after the fact (a typical suggestion is to sell protections and utilize the returns to purchase filed or variable annuities).

Goodness, and one reward tip: If somebody guarantees a venture return that is unnaturally high or consistent, the admonition caution should begin sounding.

- give a disclaimer of not-duty

This book in parts or entire remains the property of the purchaser who claims the copyright from this time forward, and not me

Principal OR TECHNICAL ANALYSIS, WHAT IS THE BEST?

Principal versus Specialized Analysis: An Overview

Central investigation and specialized examination, the significant ways of thinking with regards to moving toward the business sectors, are at far edges of the range. The two strategies are utilized for investigating and anticipating future patterns in stock costs, and, similar to any speculation technique or theory, both have their promoters and foes.

Basic Analysis

Basic examination is a strategy for assessing protections by endeavoring to gauge the inborn estimation of a stock. Essential experts study everything from the general economy and industry conditions to the money related condition and the executives of organizations. Income, costs, resources, and liabilities are terrifically significant qualities to central investigators.

Specialized Analysis

Specialized investigation contrasts from crucial examination in that the stock's cost and volume are the main sources of info. The center supposition that will be that every single realized key are figured into the cost. In this manner there is no compelling reason to give close consideration to them. Specialized investigators don't endeavor to gauge a security's natural worth, in any case, rather, utilize stock graphs to recognize examples and patterns that recommend what a stock will do later on.

The most prominent types of specialized investigation are straightforward moving midpoints, backing and obstruction, pattern lines, and force based markers.

Central examination and specialized investigation are the significant ways of thinking with regards to moving toward the business sectors.

Straightforward Moving Averages

Straightforward moving midpoints are pointers that help evaluate the stock's pattern by averaging the everyday cost over a fixed period. Purchase and sell sign are produced when a shorter span moving normal crosses a more drawn out term one.

Backing and obstruction use value history. Backing is characterized as territories where purchasers have stepped in previously, while opposition comprises of the zones where venders have obstructed value advance. Professionals hope to purchase at help and sell at obstruction.

Pattern lines are like help and obstruction, as they give characterized section and leave focuses. Notwithstanding, they contrast in that they are projections dependent on how the stock has exchanged the past. They are regularly used for stocks moving to new highs or new lows where there is no value history.

The Difference among Fundamental and Technical Analysis

Basically, the central examination plans to decide the characteristic incentive by taking a gander at the quality of the business, money related investigator, and the working condition, including macroeconomic occasions. Specialized examination investigates past market execution by taking a gander at the diagram action of value developments, volume, moving midpoints, and the measurements of different results. Central examination accept the productive market hypothesis holds over the long haul and endeavors to exploit wasteful aspects in the short run.

Specialized investigation expect essentials are as of now estimated in and attempts to discover designs that lead to results with high probabilities of happening. Specialized examination additionally catches the mental parts of the market in the survey of past examples, while principal investigation neglects to factor in financial specialist brain research however accepts basics will control in the long haul with the goal that transient mental blips will address themselves. When all is said in done, there are contrasts in the sorts of financial specialists that incline toward a particular kind of examination. Professionals are typically progressively momentary dealers commonly, diverging from the long haul see fundamentalists by and large take.

Connection Between Technicals and Fundamentals

Do basics drive technicals or a different way? In the short run, solid basics don't generally show solid specialized examples or the other way around. Regularly, technicals can keep on following a solid or frail example when basics are at defining moments, which may lead them to be out of match up. Moreover, technicals can be out of match up with essentials when there is a stun to a stock, either positive or negative.

Stocks will in general pursue technicals in the short run except if there is an unanticipated stun. For instance, there are times when stocks start moving before another material exposure winds up open. Missing insider trading or ill-advised exposures by not following Regulation D, specialized examiners state you can react progressively to stock and not need to hang tight for the following announcing date or news divulgence on the grounds that the outlines as of now decipher advertise conclusion, so following the diagrams will prompt higher benefits.

Specialized investigators accept that stocks move even without revelations since providers, contenders and representatives, and all their loved ones, put resources into organizations and without requiring inside data, get a feeling of how the organization is faring. These purchasing and selling exercises characterize the stock diagram and design and mirror the continuous stock conduct.

Now and again when the market is astounded by another divulgence, the graphs may come up short, in any event at first, and assessing the basics may prompt since a long time ago run benefits by exploiting present moment mispricing when an unexpected makes the business sectors blow up. News is impermanent and may emphatically or contrarily sway the stock's basics, so following the essentials after a stun might be increasingly judicious. In the wake of, utilizing specialized investigation may give the chance to exploit an adjustment or bounce back after the news is assimilated. In this way, regardless of whether the two have been out of match up in the short run, technicals, and basics ought to be in a state of harmony over the long haul. That is on the grounds that, over the long haul, basics should win and drive the technicals.

Time Horizon

Venture time skyline frequently directs when specialized or basic examination bodes well. Since at purposes of affectation it gives the idea that technicals and essentials are frequently out of match up, venture opportunity skyline regularly becomes possibly the most important factor. It is for the most part accepted that transient financial specialists pursue technicals while long haul speculators are happy to withstand the everyday "blips" and pursue essentials. For instance, in the event that you accept that hereditarily changed seeds are the eventual fate of cultivating, than you will most likely put resources into a significant organization—Monsanto, for instance—and are happy to stick with it in spite of any transient commotion the stock may involvement.

Diminishing Shortcomings

Pundits contend that crucial examination can prompt ill-advised valuations and in this way inappropriate speculation choices on the grounds that the data is, generally, in reverse looking. Budget summary investigation, 10Q and 10K editorials, and macroeconomic conditions center around what previously occurred. Financial specialists utilize this data to show anticipated future outcomes. The issue is that gauging is exceptionally abstract, depends on the organization supervisory group's desires and divulgences, and can be here and there an inevitable outcome. "Trash in, trash out" is a term regularly utilized related to the displaying related with crucial investigation's characteristic worth assurance.

Then again, pundits of the specialized examination believe that diagram examples work until they fizzle, and the disappointment of the example may not generally be unsurprising from following the past example, particularly if there is an unexpected stun. One approach to reduce the weaknesses of the two techniques is to utilize them together to catch the best parts of both. Major examination ought to be utilized to figure out which stocks or areas are destined to perform all around dependent on a solid macroeconomic condition and friends or part explicit tasks. Specialized examination would then be able to be utilized to choose when to purchase or sell by giving passage and leave focuses dependent on moving midpoints, volume, and value patterns.

By utilizing the two procedures together, positions can be taken in on a very basic level solid organizations while abstaining from becoming tied up with stocks that have just kept running up and are exaggerated. Specialized examination can enable you to abstain from purchasing high or selling low, a marvel which regularly happens when brain science begins to govern trading.

Crucial and specialized examination doesn't need despite what might be expected or held inside limits. On occasion there might be a solitary marker that gives data to both the specialist and fundamentalist. For instance, value instability is a significant specialized marker of risk—the more noteworthy the unpredictability, the more prominent the risk. This might be a main marker that the basics are evolving. Accordingly, both would concede to the purchase/sell choice.

The Bottom Line

Here and there speculators like to categorize themselves into one sort of venture style, yet being available to consolidating styles may give the best chance to make the most benefit. Specialized and crucial investigations don't need to be utilized alone however can be utilized together to draw a total venture picture. Basics might be utilized to recognize fitting targets, while techniques can be utilized to settle on the trading choices. Together, these strategies can create a juncture of data that ought to give a superior venture opportunity than either utilized alone.

Contrasts between Fundamental Analysis and Technical Analysis

Coming up next are a portion of the contrasts among major and specialized examination.

Specialized Analysis versus Major Analysis

1. Reason:

Major Analysis: It looks to conjecture stock costs based on financial, industry and friends insights. In any case, the most significant factors considered in choosing stock costs are profit and profits.

Specialized Analysis: It mostly centers around inward market information.

2. Long haul and Short-term Price Movement:

Central examination: It looks to anticipate long haul estimations of protections. For the most part, the fundamentalist is a moderate who contributes his assets for a long haul. Long haul financial specialists purchase a high profit paying stock and hold it for a long time through market variances.

Specialized Analysis: The specialized investigation decides the momentary value developments of the protections. The specialist is a merchant who purchases and undercuts protections for term benefits. He doesn't trust in purchasing and holding of protections. He offers significance to add up to returns, i.e., the acknowledged value less the value paid, in addition to profit got.

3. Estimation of Share

Basic Analysis: The major examiner assesses the characteristic estimation of offers and buys them when their market cost is not exactly the inherent worth. He sells the offers when the market estimation of offers is more than the natural worth and gains benefit. Consequently, he takes a shot at long haul premise.

Specialized Analysis: The expert accepts that there is no genuine incentive to any stock. As indicated by him, stock costs rely upon interest and supply powers which thus are administered by reasonable and nonsensical variables.

4. Finding the pattern

Central Analysis: In crucial examination, there is no degree for discovering the past pattern of offer and furthermore the vacillations in the value pattern.

Specialized Analysis: Technicians accept that past pattern will be rehashed and the present developments can be utilized for considering the future pattern. At the end of the day, in regard of all protections there are cycles and patterns which will happen over and over. Under specialized examination, diagrams and apparatuses are utilized to think about different value developments. The experts view value changes and their example mostly through cost and volume measurements and devices, for example, Dow hypothesis, Elliot Wave hypothesis, design distinguishing proof moving midpoints, advance or decay, diagramming styles, odd shares, short selling, put or call proportion, relative quality of pointers and Fibonacci levels.

5. Suppositions

Key Analysis: There are no suppositions in key investigation.

Specialized Analysis: Technical examination chips away at the premise of different suppositions which have been delineated before.

6. Basic leadership

Key examination: The key investigation cautiously considers the budget summaries, request figures, nature of the board, profit and development. At that point they judge the costs of protections. Subsequently, the essential examiners are settling on choices dependent on their own (emotional) feelings.

Specialized Analysis: It tunes in to what the market needs to state. Along these lines, the perspective available is the most significant factor in deciding stock costs.

7. Convenience

Principal examination: It distinguishes underestimated or exaggerated offers.

Specialized investigation: It is valuable in timing a purchase or sell request.

Trading brain science

What is Trading Psychology?

Trading brain research alludes to the feelings and mental express that help to direct achievement or disappointment in trade protections. Trading brain science speaks to different parts of a person's character and practices that impact their exchanging activities. Trading brain research can be as significant as different properties, for example, information, experience, and aptitude in deciding trading achievement. Control and risk taking are two of the most basic shares of trading brain science since a merchant's execution of these perspectives are basic to the accomplishment of their trading plan. While dread and ravenousness are the two most normally realized feelings related with trading brain science, different feelings that drive trading conduct are expectation and lament.

The field of dynamic trading is a difficult, quick paced condition with almost interminable potential outcomes and entanglements. The chances are apparently stacked against dynamic dealers in the commercial center, with studies proposing that as much as 80% reliably lose cash and just 1% accomplish unsurprising, long haul benefit.

With four out of five merchants indicating normal misfortunes, it's a marvel anybody is eager to seek after a vocation in the trading business. All things considered, it's not run of the mill for a person to put time and cash into a business that has an 80% possibility of coming up short. Anyway, why the appreciation for dynamic trading as a calling?

The appropriate response lies in the advantages that accomplishment in the commercial center can give to prosperous merchants. Money related autonomy, self-strengthening and a break from a sub-par vocation are a couple of advantages delighted in by the individuals who beat the chances and handle the metal ring.

Separating TRADING PSYCHOLOGY

Trading brain science can be related with a couple of explicit feelings and practices that are frequently impetuses for market trading. For a comprehension of these characteristics, think about a portion of the main models.

Covetousness is an extreme want for riches. It frequently makes brokers remain in a beneficial exchange longer than is prudent to press out additional benefits from it or to take on enormous theoretical positions. Ravenousness is most evident in the last period of positively trending markets when theory runs uncontrolled, and financial specialists go ahead despite any potential risks.

On the other hand, dread makes dealers close out positions rashly or to abstain from going for broke due to worry about noteworthy misfortunes. Dread is discernable during bear markets, and it is a strong feeling that can make dealers and financial specialists act nonsensically in their flurry to leave the market. Dread frequently transforms into a frenzy, which by and large causes huge selloffs in the market from frenzy selling.

Lament may make a dealer get into an exchange after at first passing up it on the grounds that the stock moved excessively quick. This is an infringement of trading order and regularly brings about direct misfortunes from security costs that are tumbling from pinnacle highs.

Specialized Analysis

Trading brain research is frequently significant for specialized investigators depending on diagramming strategies to drive their exchange choices. Security outlining can give an expansive exhibit of experiences on a security's development. While specialized investigation and diagramming strategies can be useful in spotting patterns for purchasing and selling openings, it requires a comprehension and instinct for market developments which is gotten from a financial specialist's trading brain science.

TIME MANAGEMENT

Time Management for Traders – Helpful Tips

There are numerous advantages of being a merchant. One of the primary reasons We adore being a dealer is about adaptability. This implies We don't need to get up right on time to get down to business, We don't have a manager to instruct us, we can take excursions at whatever point we need and we can likewise control our own time.

Numerous merchants anyway have a test in dealing with their time, since They don't have a clue how to oversee it in a viable way. In this article, We will feature a couple of approaches to deal with your time viably as a dealer.

A decent rest

A few people like to boast about resting for a couple of hours. 'I will rest soundly when I pass on', they state. Donald Trump, the United States president has consistently boasted about how he rests for three hours consistently. He contends that it is hard for an individual that rests for 8 hours to rival one who dozes for 3 hours. We have an alternate conclusion.

We trust in having a decent night rest. Rest encourages you to remain revived during the day. It additionally causes you to maintain a strategic distance from burnout that has influenced such huge numbers of individuals. The most ideal approach to deal with rest is to rest early and afterward get up right on time too.

Have objectives

One of the primary reasons why a great many people don't accomplish their time the executives goals is that they don't have objectives. Having objectives means having a lot of things that you need to accomplish inside a specific timeframe. Without objectives, you will have a test of time the board.

For example, each morning, you need to have a lot of things that you need to accomplish during the day. At the point when you have this arrangement of things, you will be at a decent position to accomplish most during a brief timeframe.

Organize

You ought to figure out how to organize your assignments. This implies you ought to consistently attempt to accomplish the most significant things first. For example, if your fundamental occupation is trading, you ought to do the best to attempt to do or design your trading early the morning. This is the place you ought to invest a ton of energy.

Set aside some effort to peruse, watch, and make your trading errands first. By doing this, you will be at a decent position to make progress. You ought to abstain from trading when you are worn out or when you have a great deal going on. This is very much clarified by the 80/20 standard (or Pareto Principle)

Go on vacation

The issue with numerous individuals is that they need to seem occupied. In any event, when they don't have anything to do, you will see them attempt and accomplish something. The test with this is profitability is profoundly diminished.

As a broker, you ought to consistently concentrate on efficiency! You ought to be content on each one hour spent well. In this way, in your trading day, you ought to have breaks.

Fun Things Traders Can Do In Their Free Times – Introduction

The life of a full-time merchant can be troublesome. A great many people who have their very own trading floors with Day Trade the World spend extended periods of time before their PCs doing examination and perusing news in quest for circumstances. In this article, I will feature a couple of fun things you can do as a broker.

Travel

Specialists prescribe that individuals go on vacation in any event once every year. This is the principle motivation behind why in numerous nations businesses are commanded to give their representatives downtime. In this way, you should set aside some effort to go with your family or companions. Going outside your nation and to nations of the monetary standards, stocks, or items you exchange can likewise be valuable to you. For instance, on the off chance that you are a cocoa dealer, you can exchange to Ivory Coast or Ghana where you will have the option to converse with the greatest cocoa bean ranchers.

Understand Books

Many books are discharged each month. As a broker, setting aside effort to peruse books on trading and account can enable you to hone your aptitudes. It is additionally prescribed that you set aside some effort to peruse books that are not identified with the business sectors. For instance, perusing books on connections can enable you to improve your connections which will cause you to have a superior time trading.

Mess around

In the event that you are a fanatic of computerized or physical games, you ought to take part in them at your extra time Physical games like soccer or sports can enable you to improve your self-perception. They can likewise enable you to improve your correspondence and fixation aptitudes. PC games like Fortnite will enable you to lessen the strains and make your life more joyful. In any case, you ought to be mindful so as not to overcompensate these exercises.

Watch Movies and Series

The substance business is considering expanded to be as organizations increase their spending. Consistently, Netflix spends more than $8 billion on substance creation. Organizations like Apple and Google are likewise expanding their spending on substance. AS a dealer, you ought to invest a great deal of energy watching fund related substance like Billions and Money Never Sleeps. These motion pictures will enable you to get familiar with the budgetary world and the dangers that support stock investments supervisors experience. Likewise, you should set aside effort to watch non-fund related substance.

Meetings

There are numerous meetings on fund that are held in numerous urban communities. These occasions are critical to you as a broker. This is on the grounds that they allow you to interface with other individuals in your industry. They additionally allow you to adapt new things and assemble your system. As you go to these occasions, your objective ought to be to grow your system, adapt new things, construct your certainty. You will be amazed about how these occasions can enable you to develop.

Stay away from disturbances

At long last, you ought to put forth a valiant effort to maintain a strategic distance from disturbances. This is a region where numerous individuals have a significant issue at. For instance, you may end up upset regarding online networking. You may wind up investing a great deal of energy visiting with companions. You may likewise be disturbed by TV arrangement and even music.

To stay away from these disturbances, you ought to put forth a valiant effort to have a decent workspace that is free from interruptions. You ought to likewise be principled enough to decrease examples of being disturbed.

Regular MISTAKES

1. "Neglect to plan and you intend to come up short"

Everybody realizes that it is very hard to accomplish something without arranging. We will let you know significantly more: it is difficult to exchange without an arrangement.

2. Not having a Stop Loss

Regardless of whether you are 100% certain about your benefit targets, you should better set a Stop Loss. The Forex market is exceptionally unstable, and dire news can prompt the turn of the exchange. In January 2015, the Swiss National Bank all of a sudden surrendered the top on the franc's an incentive against the euro, and EUR/CHF fell by 30%. This occasion shocked everybody. Numerous merchants who didn't have Stop Loss arranges set up endured extraordinary misfortunes. On the off chance that you don't have a Stop Loss, you may miss the snapshot of the turn that will prompt a catastrophe.

3. Adding to an unrewarding exchange

Here and there dealers are so certain in their trading points that they are incognizant of the truth. Envision that you opened a purchase request, yet the market descended. You, notwithstanding, are certain to the point that you made the correct thing that you increment the size of your situation with the expectation that the cost will before long turn around up. In a circumstance like you increase misfortunes. On the off chance that you have a vacant position, you lose the capacity to make unprejudiced decisions, and your activities confused. Subsequently, never add to a losing exchange.

A comparative thing happens when a merchant builds Stop Loss during an unfruitful exchange so the exchange doesn't close with a misfortune. Adhere to your underlying choice. Something else, your misfortune may turn out to be progressively noticeable. In the event that it was an off-base choice, investigate what turned out badly after the exchange shut, gain from this exchange and utilize this learning to improve an exchange next time.

4. Absence of risk the board

Brokers who don't deal with their dangers, chance losing everything. Merchants can't enable themselves to ponder benefits. You ought to consistently tally how a lot of cash you risk losing per exchange and every day. On the off chance that you keep your potential misfortunes restricted, you will have the option to remain in the market for quite a while and in this way have a lot more chances to win. Adhere to the standard: 1% chance per exchange. Nothing ought to occupy you from this standard.

5. Disregarding news discharges

Each merchant realizes that specific occasions and information discharges influence the Forex advertise. In the event that the real monetary markers vary from the conjecture levels, money sets become extremely unpredictable. Accordingly, all brokers, even the individuals who decide not to exchange on the news, need to consider the news. Overlooking the news is a genuine misstep that can be effectively maintained a strategic distance from on the off chance that you plan your exchanges and counsel the monetary schedule.

6. Associated sets

Brokers regularly attempt to take numerous day exchanges, yet a significant number of them don't consider cash relationships. It might appear you have great opportunities to procure cash on a few sets however be cautious: on the off chance that you see a comparative exchange arrangement numerous sets, they are likely related. So it implies you can win or lose on every one of them simultaneously. For instance, USD/CHF and USD/JPY have a huge direct connection: when the first goes up, the subsequent one will probably fortify also. Along these lines, when you purchase the two sets simultaneously, you twofold your risk.

7. Attempting to retaliate for yourself

Misfortunes are hard for everybody, particularly novices, so they attempt to have a demonstration of vengeance available. Typically, vengeance exchanges are 2-3 times greater than a past losing exchange. Accordingly, they lose significantly more. Misfortunes are unavoidable. Concentrate your vitality not on the retribution trading, however, the examining of the ineffective exchange and improve it later on.

8. Lacking instruction

The absence of instruction prompts trading visual impairment and misfortunes. In the event that you need to have gainful exchanges, you ought to consistently improve your abilities. On the off chance that you will likely be an effective dealer, read instructive books, adapt new markers, and practice new techniques.

To finish up, you will commit various errors while trading. There is one all the more saying: on the off chance that you are not committing errors, at that point you are not doing anything. In any case, on the off chance that you stay away from the regular errors referenced in this article, your trading will end up fruitful quicker.

CHAPTER SEVEN
TOP TIPS FOR FOREX TRADERS

◆ ◆ ◆

Figuring out how to exchange Forex effectively can be entangled for learners. A great many people need to get rich medium-term, regardless of how unreasonable it might sound. The universe of Forex trading can be a touch of overpowering, particularly in the event that you are new to the game, and don't have a clue about the standards yet. You have to plunge your toes in before you go any more profound. Fortunately we have your back! We've aggregated a rundown of 20 Forex tips for apprentices to help you along your trading venture 2019. In the event that you as of now have involvement with Forex trading, it's in every case great to recall the nuts and bolts.

1. Pick Your Broker Wisely

Picking the correct agent is a large portion of the fight. Take as much time as is needed to check surveys and suggestions. Ensure the agent you pick is dependable and suits your trading character. Keep in mind, there are heaps of phony dealers out there who will just hold you up. Go for an approved intermediary with a permit.

2. Make Your Own Strategy

No rundown of cash trading tips is finished in the event that it doesn't make reference to systems. One of the most widely recognized errors novice dealers make isn't making an activity plan. Make sense of what you need to escape trading. Having an unmistakable ultimate objective as a top priority will help with your trading discipline.

3. Learn Step-by-Step

Similarly as with each new useful learning action, trading expects you to begin with the nuts and bolts, and move gradually until you comprehend the playing field. Start by contributing little totals of cash, and remember the familiar proverb 'moderate however consistent successes the race'.

4. Assume Responsibility for Your Emotions

Try not to give your feelings a chance to divert you. It tends to be troublesome now and again, particularly after you've encountered a losing streak. Be that as it may, keeping a level head will enable you to remain reasonable, so you can settle on equipped decisions. At whatever point you let your feelings improve of you, you open yourself to superfluous dangers. Practicing risks the executives inside your trading will assist you with minimizing the dangers.

5. Stress Less

This is one evident Forex tip – in light of the fact that it is. Be that as it may, prepare to have your mind blown. Trading under pressure for the most part prompts unreasonable choices, and in live trading, that will cost you cash. In this manner, recognize the wellspring of your pressure and attempt to dispense with it, or possibly limit its effect on you. Take a full breath and spotlight on something different. Each individual has their method for conquering pressure – some tune in to old style music, while others work out. Tune in to your emotional wellness and realize what works best for you.

6. Careful discipline brings about promising results

Of all the Forex deceives and tips for novices, this is the most significant. You are probably not going to prevail at anything on your first attempt. Just steady trading practice can yield reliably top outcomes. Be that as it may, you most likely would prefer not to lose cash while learning the rudiments. Fortunately for you, trading on a demo account costs nothing to liberate up and is to utilize!

7. Brain research is Key

Each merchant is a therapist on the most fundamental level. At the point when you're arranging your best course of action, you need to dissect showcase developments and audit your own brain science. You have to ask yourself inquiries, for example,

- Did I give indications of affirmation inclination?
- Did I make an exchange out of dissatisfaction?
- What caused me to pick that specific money pair?

Acing your brain science will shield you from numerous misfortunes along the trading advancement way.

8. No Risk, No Success

Not even Forex trading tips and deceives can promise you achievement. At the point when you choose to turn into a broker, you ought to have just acknowledged the plausibility of disappointment. In the event that you didn't – here's a rude awakening. You won't make productive exchanges 100% of the time. Try not to give false commercials a chance to get in your mind, either. Rather, be practical about your Forex trading techniques and objectives.

9. Tolerance is a Virtue

With regards to trading, this familiar adage isn't only a prosaism. Genuine progress is rarely prompt. It's the aftereffect of steady work and arranging. Numerous learner brokers search for a simple, quick way to benefit. Try not to – it doesn't exist!

Every day you exchange, there's another exercise to be scholarly. Take a gander at the Forex market and remember every one of the tips you have learned. Start investigating news, patterns, and monetary procedures, and don't disregard the Forex nuts and bolts. In particular, study, at that point practice and afterward study some more. Rehash this procedure frequently, and you will be well on your approach to completely understanding the business sectors.

Examining will require a great deal of time and exertion, yet it will satisfy over the long haul. First of all, Admiral Markets offers the open door for dealers to profit by free instruction focus that offers Forex tips, just as, a scope of articles and instructional exercises offering tips, stunts, systems, and the sky is the limit from there, for a wide range of trading.

Before you enter any market as a merchant, you have to have some thought of how you will settle on choices to execute your exchanges. You should realize what data you should settle on the fitting choice on entering or leaving an exchange. A few people take a gander at the hidden essentials of the economy just as a diagram to decide the best time to execute the exchange. Others utilize just specialized investigation. Whichever philosophy you pick, be steady, and be certain your strategy is versatile. Your framework should stay aware of the changing elements of a market.

11. Take Breaks

An extraordinary Forex tip to pursue day by day is to remove time from your PC, particularly during upsetting trading sessions. At the point when you have a few PC windows open and numerous information streams to examine, you can normally feel constrained. For this situation, it's smarter to go for a split and stroll away for some time. Give yourself some an opportunity to gather your musings. At the point when you come back to your work area, you'll be more quiet and ready to concentrate better.

12. Patterns are Good for You

One especially significant Forex market tip to pursue is to find out about patterns. The capacity to spot patterns is a significant one. While we don't suggest getting on board with the pattern temporary fad without fail, however by and large disregarding the pattern is a catastrophe waiting to happen. Patterns can demonstrate to you what is coming, so you can professional effectively modify your trading, as opposed to responding when it's past the point of no return.

13. Look for Competitive Conditions

It's critical to pick choice help conditions and get great spreads. In case you're thinking about trading with Admiral Markets, there are a scope of various alternatives accessible. Why not read progressively about them in our account types area?

14. Plan in Advance

Forex trading isn't a bet – it's a vital game. Cautiously ascertain your best course of action before you act. You can start defining an arrangement by posing yourself some difficult inquiries, for example,

- Have I represented the likelihood that I may lose?
- What's my arrangement B for the various sorts of situations that may emerge?

To be fruitful at Forex trading, you need to expect the unforeseen.

In case you're a tenderfoot merchant searching for a spot to get familiar with the intricate details of Forex trading, our Forex 101 Online Trading Course is the ideal spot for you! Figure out how to exchange only 9 exercises, guided by an expert trading master. Snap the standard underneath to enroll for FREE!

15. Know the Charts

You will exchange on a wide range of business sectors and should rapidly comprehend the data you dissect for each exchange. There are various instruments accessible to merchants that make trading simpler, however nothing is additional time-productive than outlines. Graphs furnish you with quick access to numerically-overwhelming information as a straightforward visual, so you don't need to look through it. We urge you to become familiar with Forex outlines and how to utilize them, by perusing our related articles:

16. Try not to Run out of Chances

Enthusiasm is great, however there is an utmost to everything. In the event that you exchange excessively, you are most likely hurting your odds of making progress. Why? Since overtrading for the most part prompts debilitated concentration and imprudent exchanges. As you build up your trading plan, demonstrate the most extreme measure of exchanges you will make every day or week.

17. Eagerness Leads to Risks

Eagerness can make you accept superfluous dangers also. Set the most extreme misfortune and wanted benefit inside your trading plan. At the point when you hit this level, stop and don't go for another exchange. With regards to subsidize the board, this is one of the most significant Forex tips and deceives to pursue.

18. Use Stop-Losses

Our Forex day by day tips don't simply concentrate on general proposals. We additionally need to specify significant apparatuses, for example, the exceptionally appraised stop-misfortune. Not setting a stop-misfortune is essentially giving you a reason to keep a terrible position open (since you're trusting that the circumstance improves). Be that as it may, awful circumstances once in a while improve, and neither will your capital in the event that you don't astute up quick.

An accurately put stop-misfortune takes out the danger of losing the majority of your cash on a solitary awful exchange. The stop-misfortune is particularly helpful when you don't be able to close positions physically. To discover progressively about stop-misfortunes, try to look at the accompanying instructive articles:

19. Investigate Your Trades

Another day by day Forex tip to pursue is to keep a diary of your trading movement. This will enable you to screen your exhibition and discover designs inside your trading. Essentially, it's simpler to gain from past missteps when they are written down. Keeping a diary likewise improves your order. Make certain to record everything and speak the truth about it, as you must be your own greatest pundit.

20. Trial

One of the fundamental tips for Forex trading is to deftly alter your procedure. Be eager to evaluate new things and consistently expect to improve your trading. The FX market is continually advancing thus should you. For example, the MetaTrader 4 Supreme Edition (MT4SE) module is free for all live and demo accounts, presenting to you the most exceptional apparatuses to improve your trading background. With MT4SE, trading is made simpler with the utilization of highlights, for example, the smaller than expected terminal, the exchange terminal, the tick outline dealer, the marker bundle, the trading test system, and the little graph.

Last Thoughts

Try not to let Forex money trading scare you into surrendering, when it feels like the chances are against you. Rather, attempt to recollect that Forex achievement depends on a blend of planning and willfulness. As referenced in our Forex Trading Golden Rules article, "FX trading takes steady control to yield achievement". These Forex tips and deceives will enable you to get ready – the rest is up to you!

Picking A BROKER

Essential Things to Consider When Choosing a Forex Broker

The retail Forex market is focused to such an extent that simply considering filtering through all the accessible intermediaries can give you a significant cerebral pain. Picking which Forex specialist to exchange with can be a staggering errand particularly in the event that you don't have the foggiest idea what you ought to search for.

In this area, we will examine the characteristics you should search for when picking a Forex merchant.

1. Security

The above all else trademark that a decent representative must have is an elevated level of security. All things considered, you're not going to hand more than a huge number of dollars to an individual who just claims he's genuine, isn't that so? Luckily, checking the validity of a Forex merchant isn't hard. There are administrative offices everywhere throughout the world that different the reliable from the false.

The following is a rundown of nations with their comparing administrative bodies:

• United States: National Futures Association (NFA) and Commodity Futures Trading Commission (CFTC)

- United Kingdom: Financial Conduct Authority (FCA) and Prudential Regulation Authority (PRA)
- Australia: Australian Securities and Investment Commission (ASIC)
- Switzerland: Swiss Federal Banking Commission (SFBC)
- Germany: Bundesanstalt für Finanzdienstleistungsaufsicht (BaFIN)
- France: Autorité des Marchés Financiers (AMF)
- Canada: Investment Information Regulatory Organization of Canada (IIROC)

Before THINKING of placing your cash in a merchant, ensure that the agent is an individual from the administrative bodies referenced previously.

2. Exchange Costs

Regardless of what sort of cash broker you are, similar to it or not, you will consistently be dependent upon exchange costs.

Each and every time you enter an exchange, you should pay for either the spread or a commission so it is just normal to search for the most reasonable and least expensive rates.

Some of the time you may need to forfeit low exchange for a progressively dependable intermediary.

Ensure you know whether you need tight spreads for your sort of trading, and afterward survey your accessible alternatives. It's tied in with finding the right harmony among security and low exchange costs.

3. Store and Withdrawal

Great FX representatives will enable you to store reserves and pull back your income bother free.

Specialists truly have no motivation to make it difficult for you to pull back your benefits on the grounds that the main explanation they hold your assets is to encourage trading.

Your specialist just holds your cash to make trading simpler so there is no explanation behind you to experience serious difficulties getting the benefits you have earned. Your dealer should ensure that the withdrawal procedure is fast and smooth.

4. Trading Platform

In online Forex trading, most trading action occurs through the dealers' trading stage. This implies the trading foundation of your specialist must be easy to understand and stable.

When searching for a dealer, consistently check what its trading stage brings to the table.

Does it offer free news channel? What about simple to-utilize specialized and graphing devices? Does it present you with all the data you should exchange appropriately?

5. Execution

It is compulsory that your dealer fills you at the most ideal cost for your requests.

Under ordinary economic situations (for example typical liquidity, no significant news discharges or shock occasions), there truly is no explanation behind your specialist to not fill you at, or exceptionally near, the market value you see when you click the "purchase" or "sell" button.

For instance, expecting you have a steady web association, in the event that you click "purchase" EUR/USD for 1.3000, you ought to get filled at that cost or inside smaller scale pips of it. The speed at which your requests get filled is significant, particularly in case you're a hawker.

A couple of pips contrast in cost can make that a lot harder on you to win that exchange.

6. Client support

Specialists aren't impeccable, and subsequently you should pick a handle that you could undoubtedly contact when issues emerge.

The fitness of representatives when managing investments or specialized help issues is similarly as significant as their exhibition on executing exchanges.

Dealers might be caring and accommodating during the trade opening procedure, yet have awful "after deals" support.

Investment Details

Each Forex intermediary has distinctive investment contributions, including:

Influence and Margin: Forex members approach an assortment of influence sums relying upon the dealer, for example, 50:1 or 200:1. Influence is a credit reached out to edge account holders by their specialists. For instance, utilizing 50:1 influence, a broker with an investment size of $1,000 can hold a place that is esteemed at $50,000. Influence works in a broker's support with winning situations since the potential for benefits is significantly improved. Influence can, be that as it may, rapidly devastate a dealer's investment since the potential for misfortunes is amplified also. Influence ought to be utilized with alert.

Commissions and Spreads: A specialist profits through commissions and spreads. An expedite that utilizations commissions may charge a predetermined level of the spread, the contrast between the offer and solicit cost from the Forex pair. In any case, numerous merchants promote that they charge no commissions, and rather profit with more extensive spreads. For instance, the spread could be a fixed spread of three pips (a pip is the base unit of value change in Forex), or the spread could be variable relying upon market instability. An EUR/USD statement of 1.3943 - 1.3946 has a three-pip spread. That implies that when a market member purchases at 1.3946, the position has just lost three pips of significant worth since it must be sold promptly for 1.3943. The more extensive the spread, at that point, the more troublesome it tends to be to make a benefit. Well known trading pairs, for example, the EUR/USD and GBP/USD will normally have more tightly spreads than the more meagerly exchanged sets.

Introductory Deposit: Most Forex accounts can be subsidized with a little starting store, even as low as $50. With influence, obviously, the purchasing force is a lot more noteworthy than the base store, which is one explanation Forex trading is appealing to new brokers and financial specialists. Numerous specialists offer standard, small and smaller scale accounts with fluctuating beginning store prerequisites.

Cash Pairs Offered

While there are a lot of monetary forms accessible for trading, just a couple get most of the consideration, and in this way, exchange with the best liquidity. The "majors" are the U.S. dollar/Japanese yen (USD/JPY), the Euro/U.S. dollar (EUR/USD), the U.S. dollar/Swiss franc (USD/CHF) and the British pound/U.S. dollar (GBP/USD). An agent may offer a colossal choice of Forex sets, however what is most significant is that they offer the pair(s) in which the broker or financial specialist is intrigued.

CHAPTER EIGHT

STARTER TIPS FOR NEW TRADERS

◆ ◆ ◆

Like beginning any vocation, there is a long way to go when you're a day trading apprentice. Here are a few hints to guide you the correct way as you start your voyage. These tips will get you set up with the best possible gear and programming, help you choose what to exchange and when to trade, demonstrate to you how much capital you need, how to oversee risk, and how to rehearse an trading technique successfully.

Picking a Day Trading Market

As an apprentice informal investor, you may as of now have a market as a primary concern that you need to exchange. An informal investor's main responsibility is to discover a rehashing design (or that rehashes enough to make a benefit) and afterward abuse it.

Stocks are the portions of the organizations, for example, Walmart (WMT) and Apple (AAPL). In the Forex advertise, you're trading monetary forms, for example, the euro and US dollar (EUR/USD). There is a wide collection of fates accessible to exchange, and prospects are frequently founded on items or lists. In the fates showcase, you could exchange unrefined petroleum, gold or S&P 500 developments.

One market isn't superior to another. It comes down to what you need to exchange, and what you can manage. The Forex market requires minimal cash-flow to day exchange. You can begin with as meager as a couple of hundred dollars, albeit beginning with at any rate $500 is suggested.

Trading certain prospects markets, for example, the S&P 500 E-smaller than normal (ES), which is an extremely well known day trading fates contract, requires just $1,000 to begin. Beginning with in any event $2,500 is prescribed, however.

Stocks require at any rate $25,000 to day exchange, making them a progressively capital-concentrated alternative. While progressively capital is required to day exchange stocks, that doesn't aggravate it a superior or market than the others. Be that as it may, on the off chance that you don't have $25,000 to exchange (and can't keep up your account balance above $25,000), at that point stocks likely aren't the greatest day trading market for you. In the event that you have more than $25,000, at that point stocks are a suitable day trading market.

All business sectors offer phenomenal benefit potential. In this way it regularly boils down to how a lot of capital you have to begin. Pick a market, that way you can begin concentrating your training on that market, and not burning through your time learning things about different markets which may not be of assistance in your picked market.

Try not to attempt to ace all business sectors on the double. This will isolate your consideration and making cash may take longer. When you figure out how to profit in one market, it is simpler to adjust to learn different markets. Thus, be quiet. You don't have to gain proficiency with all business sectors without a moment's delay. You can learn different markets later on the off chance that you want.

Gear and Software for Day Trading Beginners

To day trade you need a couple of essential devices:

- A PC or workstation. Having two screens is best, yet not required. The PC ought to have enough memory and a quick enough processor that when you run your trading program (talked about later) there is no slacking or crashes. You needn't bother with a first class PC, yet you would prefer not to modest out either. Programming and PCs are always showing signs of change, so ensure your PC is staying aware of the occasions. A moderate PC can be exorbitant when day trading, particularly on the off chance that it crashes while you are in exchanges, makes you miss exchanges, or its gradualness makes you stall out in exchanges.

- A dependable and generally fast web association. Informal investors ought to use at any rate a Cable or ADSL type web association. Paces differ over these kinds of administrations, so take a stab at in any event a mid-run web bundle. The slowest speed offered by your internet service may carry out the responsibility, however on the off chance that you have numerous website pages and applications running (that utilization the web), at that point you may see your trading stage isn't refreshing as fast as it should, and that can cause issues. Start with a mid-extend web bundle, and give it a shot. You can generally change your web speed later if necessary. On the off chance that your web goes down a great deal, that is an issue. Check whether there is a progressively solid internet service. Day trading isn't prescribed with a sporadic web association.

- A trading stage fit to your market and style of day trading. At the point when you are simply beginning, finding the ideal stage isn't your objective. Download a few trading stages and give them a shot. Since you are a tenderfoot, you won't have a well-created trading style yet. Thusly, your trading stage may periodically change all through your profession, or you may adjust how it is set up to oblige your trading progress. NinaTrader is a well-known day exchanging stage for prospects and Forex dealers. There are heaps of stock trading stages. Eventually, evaluate a not many that your specialist offers and see which you like best.

- A representative. Your agent offices your exchanges, and in return charges you a commission or expense on your exchanges. Informal investors need to concentrate on low-expense merchants since high commission expenses can destroy the productivity of a day trading methodology. All things considered, the most reduced expense dealer isn't in every case best. You need a facilitate that will be there to offer help on the off chance that you have an issue. A couple of pennies extra on a commission is justified, despite all the trouble if the organization can spare you hundreds or thousands of dollars when you have a PC emergency and can't escape your exchanges. Significant banks, while they offer trading accounts, regularly aren't the best choice for informal investors. Expenses are regularly higher at significant banks, and littler merchants will normally offer progressively adaptable charge and commission structures to informal investors.

When to Day Trade

As an informal investor, both as a learner and a genius, your life is focused on consistency. One approach to create consistency is to exchange during that hours every day.

While some time or another merchants exchange for an entire ordinary session (9:30 a.m. to 4 p.m. EST, for instance, for the US financial exchange), most exchange for a part of the day. Trading just a few hours out of every day is very regular among informal investors. Here are the hours you'll need to concentrate on.

- For stocks, the best time for day trading is the first to two hours after the open, and the most recent hour before the nearby. 9:30 a.m. to 11:30 a.m. EST is a two hour time frame you need to get the hang of trading. This is the most unstable time, offering the greatest value moves and most benefit potential. The most recent hour of the day, 3 p.m. to 4 p.m. EST is additionally commonly a decent time for trading, as some sizable moves happen then as well. On the off chance that you just need to exchange for an hour or two, exchange the morning session.

- For day trading fates, around the open is an extraordinary time to day exchange. Dynamic prospects see some trading action nonstop, so great day trading openings commonly start somewhat sooner than in the financial exchange. On the off chance that day trading fates center around trading between 8:30 a.m. what's more, 11 a.m. EST. Fates markets have authority closes at various occasions, however the most recent hour of trading a prospects contract likewise commonly offers sizable moves for informal investors to benefit from.

- The Forex market exchanges 24-hours every day during the week. The EUR/USD is the most mainstream day trading pair. It commonly observes the most unpredictability somewhere in the range of 0600 and 1700 GMT. Informal investors should exchange inside these hours. 1200 to 1500 GMT regularly observes the greatest value moves, so this is an exceptionally prominent and dynamic time for informal investors. During this time both London and the US markets are open, trading the euro and the US dollar.

As an informal investor, you don't have to exchange throughout the day. You will presumably discover more consistency by just trading a few hours per day.

Deal with Your Day Trading Risk

You've picked a market, have gear and programming arrangement, and now and then comprehend what is useful for day trading. Before you even start pondering trading, you have to realize how to control chance. Informal investors should control risk in two different ways: exchange risk and every day chance.

- Trade risk is the amount you are happy to chance on each exchange. Preferably, risk 1% or less of your capital on each exchange. This is cultivated by picking a section point and after that setting a stop misfortune, which will get you out of the exchange in the event that it starts going a lot against you. The risk is likewise influenced by how enormous of a position you take, along these lines, figure out how to compute the best possible position size for stocks, Forex, or prospects. Calculating your position size, your entrance cost, and your stop misfortune value, no single exchange should open you to in excess of a 1% misfortune in capital.

- Also, control your day by day chance. Similarly as you don't need a solitary exchange to make a ton of risk on your investment (subsequently the 1% rule), you additionally don't need one day to destroy your week or month. In this way, set an everyday misfortune limit. One plausibility is to set it at 3% of your capital. On the off chance that you are gambling

1% or less on each exchange, you would need to lose three exchanges or more (without any champs) to lose 3%. With a sound technique, that shouldn't occur regularly. When you hit your day by day top, quit trading for the afternoon. When you are reliably gainful, set your everyday misfortune limit equivalent to your normal winning day. For instance, on the off chance that you ordinarily make $500 on winning days, at that point you are permitted to lose $500 on losing days. On the off chance that you lose more than that, quit trading. The rationale is that we need to keep every day misfortunes little so the misfortune can be effectively recovered by a regular winning day.

Rehearsing Strategies For Day Trading Beginners

At the point when you start, don't attempt to get the hang of everything about trading immediately. You don't have to know everything. As an informal investor, you just need one system that you execute over and over.

An informal investor's responsibility is to discover a rehashing design (or that rehashes enough to make a benefit) and afterward misuse it.

You needn't bother with a higher education or expert assignment, nor do you have to peruse many books, to do that.

Discover one procedure that gives a technique to passage, setting a stop misfortune, and taking benefits. At that point, get down to business on actualizing that technique in a demo account.

This implies you can rehearse throughout the day in the event that you need, in any event, when the market is shut.

Regardless of which market you exchange, open a demo account and start rehearsing your procedure. Realizing a methodology isn't equivalent to having the option to actualize it. No two days are the equivalent in the business sectors, so it takes practice to have the option to see the exchange arrangements and have the option to execute the exchanges decisively. Practice for at any rate three months before trading genuine capital. Just when you have in any event three months straight of productive demo execution should you change to live to exchange.

Remain concentrated on that solitary procedure, and just trading the market you picked, just during the time you have exchanged.

From Demo to Live Trading

Most merchants see disintegration in execution from when they change from demo trading to live to exchange. Demo trading is a decent practice ground for deciding whether a methodology is suitable, yet it can't impersonate the genuine market definitely, nor does it make the enthusiastic disturbance numerous dealers face when they put genuine cash on hold.

Hence, on the off chance that you see that your trading isn't going very well when you begin to live (contrasted with the demo), realize this is characteristic.

Start with the littlest position size conceivable when you initially start live trading, as this mitigates some tension of losing a lot of cash.

As you become progressively open to trading genuine cash, increment your position size up to the 1% limit talked about above. Additionally, ceaselessly take your concentration back to what you have drilled and actualizing your techniques correctly. Concentrating on exactness and usage will help weaken a portion of the compelling feelings that may contrarily influence your trading.

Last Word for Day Trading Beginners

Pick a market you are keen on and can bear to exchange. At that point, set yourself up with the correct gear and programming. Pick a period of day that you will day exchange, and just exchange during that time; normally, the greatest day trading times are around significant market openings and closings.

Deal with your risk, on each exchange, and every day. At that point, practice a technique again and again. You don't have to know it all to exchange benefit. You should have the option to actualize one procedure that profits.

Concentrate on winning with one technique before endeavoring to learn others. Sharpen your abilities in a demo account, however, understand that it isn't actually similar to genuine trading. At the point when you change to trading with genuine capital, a rough ride is regular for a while. Concentrate on exactness and execution to consistent your nerves.

Top Forex Trading Tips for Beginners

As a start Forex broker, you can without much of a stretch get lost, befuddled, or overpowered with all the data you are assaulted with on the web about trading. The best activity is to go slowly, figure out how to exchange appropriately from an accomplished proficient, and don't surge it.

The accompanying 10 Forex trading tips are things that I wish somebody had revealed to me when I initially started trading. Thus, in light of that, I am giving you ten of the most significant trading tips for a start (or any) dealer to ingest before beginning in the market.

10. Gain proficiency with the rudiments first

Many starting dealers take a stab at hopping directly into the market with no genuine foundation information on the business sectors they are trading. To manufacture a strong trading establishment, you have to set aside the effort to find out about how the Forex market functions (or any market you're trading) and truly get a strong comprehension of all the language, and so forth before you really make a plunge and start learning an trading system. You can pick up this information by taking my free amateurs Forex trading presentation course.

9. Learn one trading methodology, stay with it.

Probably the greatest mix-up I see starting dealers make over and over is changing trading strategies time and again. In the event that you are utilizing an intelligent, good judgment trading strategy like my value activity technique, you have to learn it and ace it before you do whatever else. In the event that you hop from technique to strategy since you think you'll locate some "Sacred goal" trading methodology, you are just working on false expectation and being nonsensical, and you will lose cash.

Additionally, don't switch techniques since you had a couple losing exchanges. Any technique will have a specific measure of failures over an example size of exchanges; this is typical and part of trading. You can't let losing exchanges influence you to an extreme; you do require cold control to exceed expectations at trading.

8. Try not to get overpowered

It's anything but difficult to feel overpowered with data and trading systems as a starting merchant; it happens to us all first and foremost. The most ideal approach to restrain this or stay away from it by and large is to discover a tutor, somebody to gain from, and piggy back off their prosperity. I have spread out the entirety of my trading methodologies for you to become familiar with my value activity trading course and as I would like to think, the best thing you can do is shut everything else out, overlook all that you've learned, and begin once again with my lessons from a fresh start and spotlight just on that until you truly recognize what you're doing.

7. Try not to oddity out when an exchange moves against you

This one is huge, in light of the fact that most merchants, particularly fledglings, go ballistic or over-respond whenever there's any hint of an exchange moving against them. This is substantially more of an issue in live trading than demo trading, because of the distinctions in feeling between them, yet it is an issue, and it should be tended to.

An exchange moving against you is NORMAL. I've had exchanges move to inside five pips of my stop misfortune and proceed to be HUGE victors after that. In the event that I had blown a gasket and finished them off before they hit my stop misfortune, I would have lost cash, however I would have lost a great deal of benefit as well. This is the principle motivation behind why you have to give your exchanges a chance to play out and not finish them off early ONLY in light of the fact that they've moved against you.

It's quite straightforward: Set your stop misfortune in an intelligent/safe spot (more on this later), deal with your position size so your dollar risk is at a level you're OK with losing, and LET THE TRADE GO. Don't small scale deal with your exchanges, simply let the market take the necessary steps, and you play a series of golf, go to the rec center or rest... at that point beware of the exchange the following day. Doing nothing with your live exchange is generally the best (and most rewarding) move, which means set and overlook it.

6. Concentrate on the value activity.

There was a period once, in all honesty when individuals exchanged without PCs. Difficult to trust I know, however it's valid. How would you figure they did that? It wasn't with RSI, MACD's, Stochastics or some computerized trading programming clearly... it was with

PRICE ACTION. They used to peruse the tape at the trades, or they would have the value developments posted up on enormous sheets to peruse and translate. They were translating value changes or value activity. This technique is the main 'characteristic' trading strategy, and it's been around since the 1700s when Japanese rice dealers created candle outlines to foresee changes in rice costs.

It works, don't over-convolute it. My extraordinary interpretation of value activity trading has functioned admirably for me, and on the off chance that you pursue what I state in my course and utilize outrageous order and intelligent deduction alongside tolerance, it can work for you as well! No compelling reason to mess up your diagrams and brain with a lot of chaotic and over-confounded markers or news occasions. I don't do it and neither should you since it's an exercise in futility, mental vitality and at last, your cash.

5. Be sensible

Maybe the hardest yet most significant thing for another dealer to do is to be reasonable. I'm heartbroken, however I need to reveal to you that you won't have the option to leave your place of employment and go work from a sea shore with a $2,000 trading account. In the event that some other site or individual is disclosing to you something like this, you have to RUN from them since they are tricksters and do not understand what they're discussing.

Would you be able to make a boatload of cash trading the business sectors? Indeed, obviously. Maybe no other calling on the planet has as a lot of upside potential as trading. Be that as it may, that comes at a lofty cost; it is difficult, at any rate not rationally simple.

You are going to experience a wide range of mental 'traps' and self-damage botches en route on your trading venture. Being grounded and sensible is the thing that will keep you on the way to trading achievement. In the event that you start getting dollar signs in your eyes, you're going to over-influence (chance excessively) and over exchange your account and lose cash as opposed to raking in tons of cash. You don't need that.

4. Try not to exchange a ton.

I've composed numerous articles on this subject, and I realize that for a significant number of you this will sadly not enlist in your brain until it's past the point of no return, yet you don't have to exchange a great deal to rake in tons of cash. To comprehend why all the more obviously, look at this article on high recurrence versus low recurrence trading.

3. Concentrate on the everyday graph

You have to figure out how to decipher and exchange the value activity on the day by day graph time allotment before you do whatever else. I'm not going to get into this excessively profoundly here, on the grounds that I have a few different articles on it which you can look at here:

- The best time allotments to exchange
- Daily graph time span; the 'Sacred goal'
- How trading day by day diagram will improve your trading results

2. Try not to put stop misfortunes excessively close

This one is enormous, and it takes most dealers some time and a ton of lost cash to make sense of it; you need to put your stop misfortunes at a 'protected' good ways from your entrance cost. On the off chance that you place them excessively close you will get halted out for a misfortune before the market truly got an opportunity to move in support of you. At the end of the day, your exchange thought may have been correct, but since you set your stop misfortune excessively close, you got halted out before the move you were foreseeing happened.

Here are several articles to assist you with stop misfortune position:

The most effective method to place stop misfortunes

The most effective method to utilize the ATR for stop misfortune position

1. Don't simply bounce in with no instruction

It's continually astounding to me what number of individuals need to risk their cash in the market without having gotten any preparation or trading training. At that point later, after they've lost a lot of cash, they choose to get some instruction. This is in reverse, it resembles attempting to fly a plane without going to flight school, at that point you crash the plane and nearly pass on, at that point after all that you choose to go to flight school... numerous merchants accomplish this equivalent thing with their trading accounts, don't be one of them!

Set aside your cash first for trading instruction; figure out how to exchange appropriately before whatever else, and the cash will at that point become 'pulled in' to you.

PIPS AND SPREAD

What is a pip?

A pip is a number worth. In the Forex advertise, the estimation of the cash is given in pips. One pip rises to 0.0001, two pips equivalent 0.0002, three pips rises to 0.0003, etc.

One pip is the littlest value change that a conversion scale can make. Most monetary standards are estimated to four numbers after the point. For instance, a five pip spread for EUR/USD is 1.2530/1.2535.

In the significant monetary standards, the cost of the Japanese yen doesn't have four numbers after the point. In USD/JPY, the cost is just given to two decimal focuses – so a statement for USD/JPY resembles this: 114.05/114.08. This statement has a three pip spread between the purchase and sells cost.

What is a Pip?

Pip is an abbreviation for "rate in point." A pip is the littlest value move that a swapping scale can make dependent on market show. Most money sets are valued to four decimal spots, and the littlest change is the last (fourth) decimal point. This is what could be compared to 1/100 of 1% or one premise point. For instance, the littlest move the USD/CAD money pair can make is $0.0001 or one premise point.

A pip is an essential idea of outside trade (Forex). Forex sets are utilized to disperse trade cites through offer and ask cites that are precise to four decimal spots. In less complex terms, Forex brokers purchase or sell a money whose worth is communicated in relationship to another cash.

For instance, a merchant who needs to purchase the USD/CAD pair would buy US Dollars and at the same time selling Canadian Dollars. On the other hand, a merchant who needs to sell US Dollars would sell the USD/CAD pair, purchasing Canadian dollars simultaneously. Dealers frequently utilize the expression "pips" to allude to the spread between the offer and solicit costs from the money pair and to show how a lot of addition or misfortune can be acknowledged from an exchange.

What Is A Pip?

KEY TAKEAWAYS

- Bid cost is the value that a dealer can sell a money pair and is lower than the ask value, which is the value that a broker can purchase a cash pair.
- The contrast among offer and ask costs is alluded to as the spread.

- The spread is normally cited in pips.

The most effective method to Calculate Pips

Development in the conversion scale is estimated by pips. Since most money sets are cited to a limit of four decimal places, the littlest change for these sets is 1 pip. The estimation of a pip can be determined by separating 1/10,000 or 0.0001 by the conversion scale.

Japanese Yen (JPY) sets are cited with 2 decimal spots, denoting a remarkable special case. For money matches, for example, the EUR/JPY and USD/JPY, the estimation of a pip is 1/100 separated by the conversion scale. For instance, if the EUR/JPY is cited as 132.62, one pip is $1/100 \div 132.62 = 0.0000754$.

Pips and Profitability

The development of a money pair decides if a merchant made a benefit or misfortune from their situations toward the day's end. A broker who purchases the EUR/USD will benefit if the Euro increments in worth comparative with the US Dollar. In the event that the merchant purchased the Euro for 1.1835 and left the exchange at 1.1901, the person in question would make $1.1901 - 1.1835 = 66$ pips on the exchange.

Presently, how about we consider a dealer who purchases the Japanese Yen by selling USD/JPY at 112.06. The merchant loses 3 pips on the exchange whenever shut down at 112.09 however benefits by 5 pips if the position is shut down at 112.01.

While the distinction looks little in the multi-trillion dollar outside trade market, increases and misfortunes can include rapidly. For instance, if a $10 million situation in this set-up is shut down at 112.01, the dealer will book a $10 million x (112.06 - 112.01) = ¥500,000 benefit. This benefit in US dollars is determined as ¥500,000/112.01 = $4,463.89.

What is the spread?

The spread is the distinction between the purchase (likewise called offer) cost and the sell (additionally called ask) cost. Two costs are given for a money pair. The spread speaks to the contrast between what the market producer provides for purchase from a merchant, and what the market creator takes to offer to a broker.

On the off chance that a dealer purchases any cash and promptly sells it – and no adjustment in the conversion scale has occurred – the merchant will lose cash. The explanation behind this is the offered cost is consistently lower than the ask cost.

For instance, the EUR/USD offer/ask money rates at your bank might be 1.2015/1.3015. This speaks to a spread of 1000 pips. This spread is high contrasted with the offered/approach money rates for online Forex financial specialists, for example, 1.2015/1.2020 – a spread of 5 pips.

When all is said in done, littler spreads are better for Forex financial specialists in light of the fact that a littler development in return rates gives them a chance to benefit from an exchange all the more effectively.

The spread is the place the market producer will profit. See simple Forex® trading highlights for data on our spreads.

Forex Scalping

Forex trading can be an intense and dynamic speculation region, where just exact data of complexities and complexities of the market can make your assets take off every day. It's imperative to recollect that there is no idiot proof money trading strategy which ensures supreme achievement. Each strategy includes dangers, and no trading framework is resistant to misfortunes.

In any case, there are a couple of cutting edge Forex trading techniques which can assist you with achieving palatable trading benefits, one of which is Forex Scalping. This system expects to make a potential benefit rapidly. Viewed as one of the most exceptional trading procedures, the possibility of this system is that trading is performed to sum things up time periods with benefits picked up as often as possible after slight moves in the Forex showcase.

It's a great and inventive Forex technique, however it requires a nitty gritty examination of the market before an exchange is advertised. This sort of cash trading agrees with risk unwilling informal investors. That being stated, numerous individuals online are still at furthest edges concerning Forex scalping. Nonetheless, everybody concurs with the central thought. The contention comes in detail – nobody can concede to it.

After broad examination, a few points of interest have been come to about the most widely recognized thoughts encompassing the strategy. Everybody appears to concur that scalping happens once merchants dispose of situations for a concise period. To what extent the period endures is the place individuals don't concur. This Forex trading procedure can possibly enable you to make critical benefits rapidly and productively. The inquiry is, how would you scalp Forex?

Exchange Forex and CFDs with Admiral Markets

Expert trading has never been more open than this moment! Chief of naval operations Markets offers proficient dealers the capacity to exchange on the Forex advertise legitimately and through CFDs with 80+ monetary forms, including Forex majors, Forex minors, outlandish sets and that's just the beginning! Open your live trading account today by tapping the flag beneath!

It includes taking out a situation for whenever under five minutes. If you don't mind note this will in general be the fundamental downside to this Forex trading system. In the event that you exchange a brief span outline, you can't make a not too bad profit for your venture. This is on the grounds that sets just go up or somewhere around a couple of pips. As you may as of now know, making more pips implies more benefit. Hence, Forex hawkers will in general exchange mass amounts.

As a rule, the further developed Forex trading aptitudes you have, the bigger your capital and the bigger your volumes are. Scalping is a generally utilized method among prepared Forex merchants. The strategy is subject to variances in money esteem, occurring in the market at specific interims consistently.

As a rule, the time between the end and opening position is short and endures just merely minutes. Benefits picked up from this position will in general be low. In any case, the all-out addition accomplished by tremendous positions can be noteworthy. Some Forex merchants exchange up to 200 situations in a day. Without a doubt, not all positions opened by dealers can make benefits for them, yet the conclusive objective is to have a general benefit by joining all positions.

One tip is that when scalping, you should put in a stop-misfortune request close to the opening cost of the situation for decreasing the misfortunes when there is variance toward the market. It is constantly prescribed that you utilize a stop-misfortune on your scalping exchanges. As this is one of the progressed Forex trading strategies, how about we abridge this system and the guidelines a dealer ought to agree to:

- Don't hold a position open for quite a while, ideally the most extreme holding time ought not surpass five minutes.
- The size of the exchange ought to be fairly enormous, as the measure of picked up pips per exchange is very little.
- The higher the quantity of every day exchanges is, the higher the odds are of being fruitful with Forex scalping.
- This procedure is legitimate for informal investors, implying that you would most likely need to invest a great deal of energy trading to accomplish results with it.

Free Live Trading Webinars With Admiral Markets

Did you realize that you can enlist for FREE to ordinary trading online classes with Admiral Markets? Gain legitimately from expert trading specialists and discover how you can discover accomplishment in the live trading markets. Find out about the best trading pointers, the most prevalent techniques, the most recent news, patterns and improvements in the business sectors, thus considerably more!

Positional Trading

This is absolutely a progressed Forex methodology, as it is utilized by the top-gaining brokers. The principle bit of leeway of this technique is that it requires much less every day consideration. Nonetheless, it must be finished effectively with a cautious long haul showcase investigation. Most Forex trading systems are performed on little league outlines, implying that most of them are day trading techniques.

Positional trading is something totally not quite the same as day trading – and it's particularly not the same as scalping. At the point when a broker beginnings trading positions, they are relied upon to hold a situation for a significant extensive stretch. It is difficult to recognize the base suggested holding time as it principally relies upon the dealer's diagram of the market, and the quantity of pips picked up.

When utilizing positional trading, one of the most progressive Forex methods, a dealer needs to do everything in totally the contrary route contrasted with Forex scalping. The exchange size will in general be fairly little in correlation with the trading capital. While scalping, you endeavor to open enormous situations, as you are hoping to make a couple of pips for each exchange. During positional exchanging, you are intending to get in excess of 100 pips, which can make your position more secure when the market varies.

To stay away from tremendous risk, a broker is prescribed to exchange just taking things down a notch, putting close to 2% of their assets at the exchange edge. Along these lines, you can undoubtedly bear the cost of going down for 20-30 pips without shutting your position. One of the primary highlights of positional trading is to guarantee that you earn back the original investment toward the finish of your exchange. Now and then you may increase a few pips for every exchange, except then still lose the assets.

How could that be? This happens on the grounds that the positions are held for half a month or even months, and in this way are a liable to swaps. Swaps are otherwise called the charge for moving your position medium-term. You may likewise discover swaps being alluded to as rollovers or rollover expenses. As it were, a dealer may open a long position on the EUR/USD money pair on 1 May, and after that dispose of their situation on 1 July, with a complete increase of 50 pips.

Be that as it may, the swaps on this money pair could be high to such an extent that a 50 pip increase won't be sufficient to make up for a 60-day rollover charge. That being stated, note that rollovers are not constantly a disservice. On some trading instruments, there are certain rollovers. This implies by really holding a position, you are benefitting as well. There is considerably another progressed Forex trading methodology known as 'convey trading,' which depends on gaining through rollovers.

To perform positional trading effectively, you surely need to have an incredible diagram of the current monetary circumstance in the nations of the monetary forms you are intending to exchange, alongside current geopolitical issues. The majority of your investigation ought to happen before you open a position, while further examination ought to for the most part be utilized for the distinguishing proof of the leave point.

NFP Trading

By and large, NFP (or Nonfarm Payrolls) is the major monetary news discharged in the US once consistently. For the most part, this kind of market news severely affects informal investors, as it can without much of a stretch change a cost of USD sets for at least 50 pips. The fundamental detriment of this trading procedure is that it is tight to the NFP discharges, so you can just utilize NFP trading once per month.

NFP resembles a progressed Forex level of scalping. A couple of hours before NFP results are set to be discharged, the market starts to vary. Your primary point here is to recognize the potential consequences of the NFPs, and after that judge how extraordinary they will be from both the past and anticipated qualities. You can watch these qualities utilizing the Forex Calendar page. You additionally need to ensure that you have enough edge to retain any conceivable market variances before the NFP results are discharged.

When the news is out, the cost of the pair may alter its course definitely. In the event that the bearing of the change is the manner in which you expected, you may increase a high number of pips in only a couple of hours. On the other hand, on the off chance that the alter occurs in the contrary course, at that point your stop-misfortune is activated. At the end of the day, NFP trading is tied in with making numerous pips out of a triumphant exchange and after that limiting your misfortunes if the expectation doesn't work out.